The author at Montsegur, walking the Cathars Way, September 2011.

Happy walking!

John W Merrill

The John Merrill Foundation & Ministry.

www.johnmerrillwalkguides.com

www.pilgrimways.co.uk

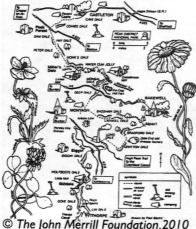

THE LIMEY WAY - 40 MILES
Created and inaugurated by John N. Merrill - May 1969.

© The John Merrill Foundation. 2010

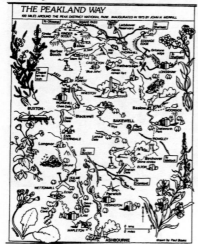

© The John Merrill Foundation. 2010

Walk the finest limestone dale walk in the Peak District -

THE LIMEY WAY

by John N. Merrill
- 40 miles from Castleton to Thorpe via twenty dales.
Guide book available from -
THE JOHN MERRILL FOUNDATION

Walk the finest long distant route in the Peak District -

THE PEAKLAND WAY

by John N. Merrill
- 100 mile circular route from Ashbourne taking in the finest places and scenery in the Peak District National Park.

Happy walking!
John N. Merrill

THE ART OF WALKING THE JOHN MERRILL WAY

1. Always set off in the clothes you plan to wear all day, given the weather conditions. Only on sudden changes in the weather will I stop and put on a waterproof or warmer clothing.

2. Set off at a steady comfortable pace, which you can maintain all day. You should end the walk as fresh as when as you started.

3. Maintain your pace and don t stop. Stopping for any period of time disrupts your rhythm and takes upwards of a mile to settle back down into the flow/ease of movement.

4. Switch off your mobile phone and music centre, and listen and enjoy the countryside - the smells of the flowers, bird song, the rustle of the leaves and the tinkling stream.

5. Ignore the mileage and ascents - don t tick off the miles, just concentrate on what the walk s goal is. To think otherwise slows you down and makes the walk a struggle rather than a joy. In a similar vein, when ascending just keep a steady pace and keep going. To stop is to disrupt the flow and make the ascent interminable.

6. Whilst a walk is a challenge to complete, it is not just exercise. You should enjoy the world around you; the flowers, birds, wildlife and nature and look at and explore the historical buildings and church s that you pass. All are part of life s rich tapestry.

7. Remember that for every mile that you walk, you extend your life by 21 minutes.

8. A journey of a 1,000 miles begins with a single step and a mile requires 2,000 strides.

The expert traveller
leaves no footprints.
Lao Tzu.

Short Circular walks on the New River & South-East Hertfordshire

by John N. Merrill

Maps, pencil sketches and photographs by John N. Merrill.

"I hike the paths and trails of the world for others to enjoy."

"The miracle of life is not to fly in the air, or walk on the water, but to walk upon the earth." CHINESE SAYING.

THE JOHN MERRILL FOUNDATION

The Short Circular Walks Series Vol. 61.

2012

THE JOHN MERRILL FOUNDATION
32, Holmesdale, Waltham Cross, Hertfordshire, England. EN8 8QY

Tel - 01992-762776 Fax - +44(0)870 131 5061
E-mail - marathonhiker@aol.com
www. johnmerrillwalkguides.com
www.pilgrimways.co.uk

A catalogue record for this book is available from the British Library.

Conceived, edited, typeset and designed by *The John Merrill Foundation*
Printed and handmade by *John N. Merrill.*
Book layout and cover design by *John N. Merrill*

© Text and photographs - by Revd. John N. Merrill HonMUniv, R.I.M.A. 2011
© Maps by Revd. John N. Merrill, HonMUniv, R.I.M.A. 2011
© Maps, Photographs & pencil sketches - John N. Merrill, HonMUniv, 2011.

ISBN 978 -1-903627-69-3
First Published - November 2005. Reprinted and enlarged - January 2012.
Special limited edition.

Typeset in Humanst521 - bold, italic, and plain 11pt, 14pt and 18pt
Main titles in 18pt .**Humanst521 Bd BT** by John Merrill in Adobe Pagemaker on a iMac.

Please note - *The maps in this guide are purely illustrative. You are encouraged to use the appropriate 1:25,000 O.S. Explorer map as detailed on each walk.*

John Merrill confirms he has walked all the routes in this book and detailed what he found. Meticulous research has been undertaken to ensure that this publication is highly accurate at the time of going to press. The publishers, however, cannot be held responsible for alterations, errors, omissions, or for changes in details given. They would welcome information to help keep the book up to date.

The John Merrill Foundation maintains the John Merrill Library and archives and administers the worldwide pubishing rights of John Merrill's works in all media formats.

Printed on paper from a 100% sustainable forest.
The John Merrill Foundation plants sufficient trees through the Woodland Trust to replenish the trees used in its publications.

The author at Montsegur, walking The Cathar Way in Southern France; September 2011.

ABOUT THE AUTHOR

Over the last 46 years John Merrill has walked over 204,000 miles, - more than ten times around the world - wearing out 116 pairs of boots in the process. He has completed a remarkable and unequalled number of marathon walks - walking more than 28 miles per day on average - including being the first person to walk around Britain - 7,000 miles - in ten months. He has walked across Europe, Africa, India, Nepal, Asia, America, and along the great trails of America and Canada. He has completed numerous Pilgrim routes to Santiago de Compostela, Canterbury, Walsingham, St. Albans and to Trondheim in Norway. Many more pilgrimages and marathons are planned. He is acknowledged as Britain's Greatest Walker.

He has written more than 380 guidebooks to his walks, most of which he prints and publishes himself. After his coast walk he realised the fame game prevented his from doing what he was destined to do, and that was to simply walk and write. He purposefully left the stage and concentrated on what he wanted to do. He does not consult anyone, promote or seek publicity; preferring to follow his own quiet spiritual path through life. This means he can write a book, on average one every month. He is not beholden to anyone, just a free spirit, with no staff, agents or editors. As a result he is not rich in money terms but in life and places walked to, a millionaire.

He is not a loner, quite the reverse, but to get the material and accomplish his walks - he who travels alone, travels fastest. And, by going alone you never forget. He is guided and has a very deep spiritual faith and has never come to any harm or put a foot wrong. The only way to be close to nature and see its huge variety is by walking; no other sport/exercise gives you that connectedness to the earth. He does no research beforehand, preferring to walk around the corner and come to a church, historic house, sacred site etc., and discover for himself their secrets. To be aware of what's next is to dampen the impact.

> " A journey of a thousand miles, begins with a single step."
> Lao Tzu (The Tao Te Ching).

I am on a long journey, which continues daily - one life is not enough.

"I cannot be defined,
No Label sticks to me,
No pigeon hole do I fit.
I am connected to everything,
I am part of the whole.
A part has no meaning on its own"
(©John Merill 17/9/2010)

My religion is simple - *"I love everything and everyone"*

On July 17th. 2010 John was Ordained as an Interfaith Minister - *"He embraces and honours all faiths."*

See - **www.pilgrimways.co.uk**   **www.interfaithfoundation.org**

CONTENTS

Forty Hall.

INTRODUCTION

I bucked the trend and moved south to Hertfordshire, since my girlfriend lived here! My first walk was from Forty Hall and was immediately impressed by the scenery and history. I wanted to know more and what became my first book on the area, I walked the River Lee Navigation - see my book, "Short Circular Walks in the River Lee Navigation". While I walked that I kept following bits of the New River Path and wanted to know more; hence this book!

But I just didn't want to explore and walk and New River path, but the countryside it passed through between the suburbs of Enfield and Hertford. Restricting myself to this narrow strip, bordered by the River Lee Navigation, I was surprised at the variety of walking here - the river of course, but the magnificent woodland, historic and unspoilt villages and abundant wildlife.

Riverside walking is tranquil and most of landscape is relatively flat, so no major climbs or descents. All can be followed at a leisurely pace while you explore the countryside on your doorstep. It is hard to say which walk I liked best, for each walk has its own character, but the walk from Hertford Heath to the mouth of the New River, holds a special place. So does the one passing through Haileybury College. The Woodland of Broxbourne area is outstanding and the fascinating places of Wormleybury and Brickendon, harp back to a peaceful era away from the hustle and bustle of modern life.

So here is a collection of rewarding and unspoilt walks, many of which explore a section of the New River, be it old or new. The final walk - 16 miles - explores the New River from Forty Hill to Islington, and is a surprisingly enjoyable walk through London suburbia. Lace on your boots; switch the mobile phone off; and tread the soft earth and listen to the natural sounds of the countryside as you walk by wood or river.

Happy walking

Alan W Merricks

7

ABOUT THE WALKS
- some general comments.

Whilst every care is taken detailing and describing the walks in this book, it should be borne in mind that the countryside changes by the seasons and the work of man. I have described the walk to the best of my ability, detailing what I have found actually on the walk in the way of stiles and signs. Obviously with the passage of time stiles become broken or replaced by a ladder stile, a small gate or a kissing gate. Signs too have a habit of being broken or pushed over - vandelism. All the route follow rights of way and only on rare occasions will you have to overcome obstacles in its path, such as a blown down tree, barbed wire fence or an electric fence. On rare occasions rights of way are rerouted and these ammendments are included in the next edition. Inns have a frustrating habit of changing their name, then back to the original one!

All rights of way have colour coded arrows; on marker posts, stiles/gates and trees; these help you to show the direction of the right of way :-

> **Yellow - Public footpath.**
> **Blue - Public bridleway.**
> **Red - Byway open to all traffic (BOAT).**
> **Black - Road used as a public path (RUPP).**

The seasons bring occasional problems whilst out walking which should also be borne in mind. In the height of summer paths become overgrown and you may have to fight your way through in a few places. In low lying areas the fields are often full of crops, and although the pathline goes straight across it may be more practical to walk round the field edge to get to the next stile or gate. In summer the ground is generally dry but in autumn and winter, especially because of our climate, the surface can be decidedly wet and slippery; sometimes even gluttonous mud!

These comments are part of countryside walking which help to make your walk more interesting or briefly frustrating. Standing in a track up to your ankles in mud might not be funny at the time but upon reflection was one of the highlights of the walk!

The mileage for each section is based on three calculations -

> **1. pedometer reading.**
> **2. the route map measured on the map.**
> **3. the time I took for the walk.**

I believe the figure stated for each section to be very accurate but we all walk differently and not always in a straight line! The time allowed for each section is on the generous side and does not include pub stops etc. The figure is based on the fact that on average a person walks 2 1/2 miles an hours but less in hilly terrain. Allow 20 minutes to walk a mile; ten minutes for 1/2 mile and five minutes for 1/4 mile. On average you will walk 2,000 strides to a mile - an average stride is 31 inches..

"For every mile you walk, you extend your life by 21 minutes"

Follow the Countryside Code.

* Be safe - plan ahead
and follow any signs.

* Leave gates and property
as you find them.

* Protect plants and animals, and take
your litter home.

* Keep dogs
under close control.

* Consider
other people.

NEW RIVER
- some brief history notes.

As many historical notice boards along the river state - It is not a river, nor is it new. It is a remarkable piece of 17th. century engineering to bring clean water to London, some 400 years ago. Originally 40 miles long from Chadwell Spring near Hertford, to the New River Head in Islington, London; close to Saddler's Wells Theatre. The "river" hugs the 100 foot contour line, often doing loops to maintain height, such as around Forty Hall and Enfield Town. Today it is 24 miles long, with the loops omitted by taking the water through pipes and tunnels. The aim behind the 100 foot contour line, was so water could then be gravity fed to the houses of the City of London.

A water channel was proposed in 1600 and an Act of 1606 basically set up the scheme. Originally Edmund Colhurst, who had proposed the channel, was to undertake the task. However concerns over financing, the council accepted an offer from Hugh Myddleton, a welshman, who was a London goldsmith and a former M.P. He agreed to finance the project himself and complete it on four years. Hugh Myddleton was knighted in October 1662 and died on December 10th. 1631 and a statue to him can be seen in Islington close to Camden Antique Market.

Work began at Chadwell Spring on April 21st. 1609 and was completed more than four years later on September 29th. 1613 - the Lord Mayor of London officially opened the waterway on this day. The cost of construction is believed to be £18,527. 0d. 1d. The "river" was basically 10 feet wide and 4 feet deep. Puddled clay was used as a liner to make it waterproof. Over its 40 mile length the water falls 18 ft. - 5 1/2 inches a mile. 157 bridges were built along its path for roads and paths across the "river".

In the first year 175 houses were using the water supply and the following year this had doubled. By 1809 it was 59,058 houses and by 1834 this had risen to 73,212. As the demand for water increased reservoirs were built at Cheshunt and the East and West Reservoirs at Stoke Newington.

The New River is still used by Thames Water Board; the river being fed mostly by the River Lee, which rises near Luton. Originally the New River was fed by the springs at Chadwell and Amwell, who combined provided a maximum of 10 megalitres a day. A statue in 1738 allowed upto 102 megalitres to be taken from the River Lee. More than century later these amounts were doubled. Today, more than 38 million gallons of water, a day, is brought to London along this "river."

For a full in depth look at the New River, see Michael Essex-Lopresti book - ***"Exploring The New River."***

Sir Hugh Myddleton Statue, Islington.

FORTY HALL, CHESHUNT AND NEW RIVER - 7 MILES

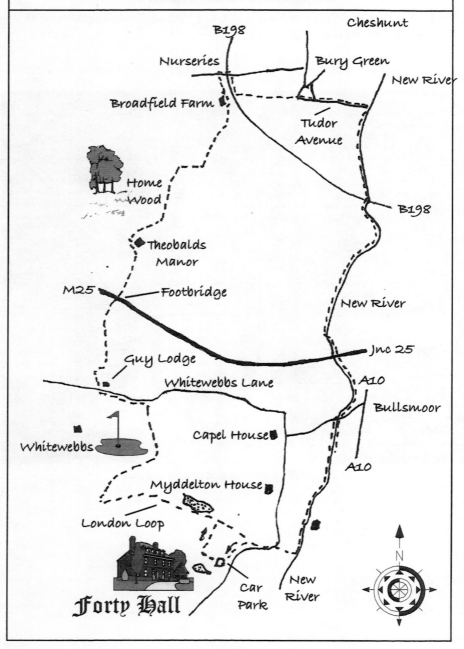

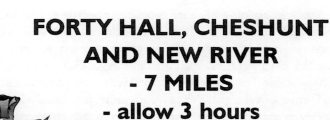

FORTY HALL, CHESHUNT AND NEW RIVER
- 7 MILES
- allow 3 hours

Basic route - Forty Hall - London Loop - New River (Old Course) - Whitewebbs Lane - Guy Lodge - M25 - Theobalds Manor - Home Wood - Broadfield Farm - B198 - Bury Green - New River - M25 - New River - London Loop - Forty Hall.

Map - O.S. 1:25,000 Explorer Series No. 174 - Epping Forest & Lee Valley.

Car park and start - Forty Hall. Grid Ref. 174/338985.

Inns - The King & Tinker, Whitewebbs Lane.

Snacks - Forty Hall.

ABOUT THE WALK - Starting from the historic Forty Hall, which is well worth a visit to see the hall and walled gardens, the walk explores the western side of suburbia. Following paths you pass Whitewebbs, cross the M25 and pass Theobalds Manor to reach the Bury Green area of Cheshunt. From here you soon head southwards along the banks of the New River, crossing the M25 and continuing to the London Loop waymarked path. This brings you back into Forty Hall. A delightful mixture of pleasant countryside and river walking.

WALKING INSTRUCTIONS - Starting from the car park beside Forty Hall, walk to the end of the car park and keep ahead for about 100 yards to a line of trees. Turn right and descend down them to the bottom to pickup a path/track which leads you to the waymarked London Loop path. Turn left along it soon passing a lake in the trees on the right, as you walk through woodland. At a fork keep left and reach a path sign - Mile & Quarter path heading to Whitewebbs Lane. Turn right over a footbridge over Turkey Brook, and keep a fence on your right and a golf course on your left. Reach a kissing gate and follow the path right, now a Local Heritage Trail, beside the Old Course of the New River. The path turns left still with a wooden fence beside and in 1/4 mile from the river, gain Whitewebbs Lane. Just before it turn left then right to follow a path paralleling the road. In 1/4 mile reach the King & Tinker Inn.

Just after and past Guy Lodge on the right, turn right as path signed - Cheshunt - over a stile. Keep to the lefthand side and soon walk along a hedged path to a stile. Continue with a fence on your left to a stile and onto a footbridge. Cross and ascend to the prominent footbridge over the M25. Cross and continue with a fence on your right and trees on the left to a track. Keep ahead along it to a lane - Oldpark Ride - opposite Theobalds Manor. Turn left then right in a few yards, as path signed, and continue to a gate. Bear right with Home Wood on your immediate left. Follow the path left beside it to its end and a hedge. Turn right along a grass path to a stile on the left. Turn left keeping the hedge on your left to stiles and onto Broadfield Farm, reached by a track. Approaching the farm bear right and left to walk around its righthand side, using stiles, and gain the concrete farm drive beyond. Follow it to a lane and turn right crossing the B198. Immediately turn right past houses on the left, as path signed, to a stile. Turn left and follow the path with a cemetery on your left to Woodside and houses of Bury Green. Turn left along Warrenfield Close and in a few yards right along Portland Drive. A few yards later beside house no. 163, turn left along Grove Path. Reaching the road - Tudor Avenue - keep straight ahead down this to its end and a kissing gate onto the New River path.

Turn right along the path with the river on your left (Cover photograph). In more than 1/4 mile cross a footbridge and continue with the river on your right. Pass under the B198 and onto a kissing gate. Continue along the river path and 3/4 mile later reach a kissing gate and New River Path sign. Keep straight ahead and cross the piped bridge of the New River over the M25. Across continue beside the river; now on your left. In 1/4 mile cross the road near Bullsmoor. Less than 1/2 mile later gain another kissing gate and lane. Turn left then right by house no. 184, and continue on the New River Path, with the river now on your right. Soon pass an overhead river clearing area, and now follow the path by a fence on your right to a kissing gate and onto a tarmaced path and the London Loop path. Turn right and soon reach Forty Hall Road with a school on your left. Cross to your left to a stile and turn left and ascend the open field on a distinct pathway back to Forty Hall Car Park.

FORTY HALL - Built in 1629 for Sir Nicholas Raynton; Lord Mayor of London and President of St. Bartholomew's Hospital. The hall, a fine Jacobean Mansion, is known for traditional compact design, plaster ceilings, panelled rooms and walled gardens. In 1787 the hall and estate were auctioned, with the hall being bought by Edmund Armstrong. By 1895 it was owned by Major Henry Bowles MP for Enfield. In 1951 Enfield Urban District Council bought the hall and grounds and converted them into a museum; a visit is highly recommended.

WHITEWEBBS, CREWS HILL AND SILVER STREET - 7 1/2 MILES

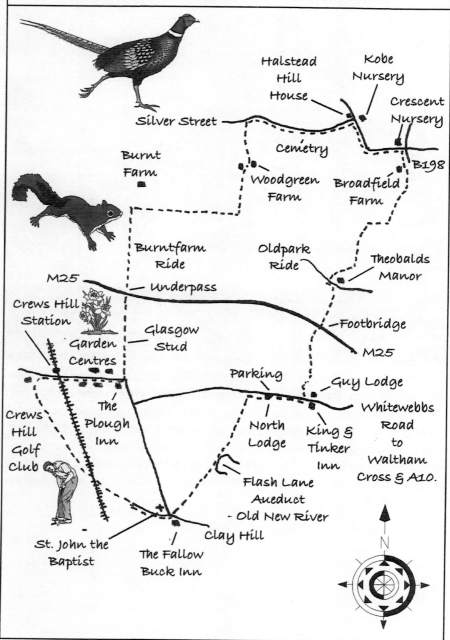

Halstead Hill House

Kobe Nursery

Crescent Nursery

Silver Street

Cemetery

B198

Burnt Farm

Woodgreen Farm

Broadfield Farm

Burntfarm Ride

Oldpark Ride

Theobalds Manor

M25

Underpass

Crews Hill Station

Garden Centres

Glasgow Stud

Footbridge

M25

Parking

Guy Lodge

Crews Hill Golf Club

The Plough Inn

North Lodge

King & Tinker Inn

Whitewebbs Road to Waltham Cross & A10.

Flash Lane Aueduct - Old New River

Clay Hill

St. John the Baptist

The Fallow Buck Inn

N

WHITEWEBBS, CREWS HILL AND SILVER STREET
- 7 1/2 MILES
- allow 3 hours.

Basic route - Whitewebbs Road - Whitewebbs Wood - Clay Hill - Crews Hill Golf Course - Crews Hill Station - Crews Hill - Glasgow Stud - M25 - Burntfarm Ride - Woodgreen Farm - Silver Street - Adath Yisroel Cemetery - Kobe Nursery - Crescent Nursery - Broadfield Farm - Oldpark Ride - M25 - Guy Lodge - Whitewebbs Road.

Map - O.S. 1:25,000 Explorer Series No. 174 - Epping Forest & Lee Valley.

Car Park and start - Whitewebbs Road; off road parking near North Lodge - Grid Ref 174/328999. Alternative start - As you pass Crews Hill Station, the walk can be started and ended here.

Inns - The King & Tinker, Whitewebbs Road. The Fallow Duck, Clay Hill. The Plough Inn, Crews Hill.

Teas - Cafe's in the Garden Centres in Crews Hill.

ABOUT THE WALK - An undulating walk through woodland and along tracks with views to central London. Despite straddling the M25 and lying between Enfield suburbs and Goff's Oak, the area is rich in wildlife. I saw numerous pheasant, grey squirrels, hares, rabbits, disturbed two woodpeckers and a jay. Crews Hill Garden Centre strip is a stark contrast to the quiet Burntfarm Track! The first part of the route is littered with inns!

17

WALKING INSTRUCTIONS - Starting from the lay-by parking area near North Lodge on Whitewebbs Road, turn left past the lodge into Whitewebbs Park. Turn right after a few yards onto the bridleway which parallels the road at first, before turning left - south-west. Follow the fenced track through Whitewebbs Wood and after 1/2 mile gain the Flash Lane Aqueduct, of the former New River. Continue straight ahead on the track with the defined river bed on your left. After a short distance it turns left and you keep ahead ascending gently the track - Flash Lane - to the road at Clay Hill; opposite is the Fallow Buck Inn.

Cross the road to the right to walk along Strayfield Road, passing St. John the Baptist church on your right. Keep straight ahead along the tarmaced road. In 1/4 mile reach a path junction and keep ahead, as path signed, on a track then path and descend to the railway line. Cross with care and follow the railed path up and into Crews Hill Golf Course. Guided by white posts on the left walk between the fairways and greens for more than 1/2 mile to the Club House and car park. Walk along its righthand side to a stile and the Crews Hill Road. Turn right and pass under the railway line with Crews Hill Station on your left. Walk down the road past the garden centres (cafe's) to where the road turns sharp right near the Plough Inn.

Turn left along the tarmaced lane. Pass Theobalds Farm House, then Glasgow Stud. Beyond it is a track and walk through the M25 underpass and keep straight ahead. Pass Tile Kiln Cottage on your left and follow the tree lined track - Burntfarm Ride - for 1/2 mile to a path crossroads. Turn right, still on a tree lined track with woodland on the right - Cattlins. Along here were numerous pheasant, grey squirrels, and a hare. Follow the undulating track and in 1/2 mile turn left, as path signed - Silver Street 0.8 km. Follow the track by the edge of the field towards Woodgreen farm; on your right are extensive views. Walk through the farm and stables and along the farm drive to Silver Street. Turn right along the quiet Silver Street and in 1/4 mile pass the Jewish Cemetery - Adath Yisroel, on your right. Pass Woodgreen Park Cottage and ascend to the road junction with Halstead Hill House on the left; opposite is Kobe Nursery.

Turn right along the lane and pass Elm Lodge on the right in 1/4 mile, where the lane turns left. In less than 1/4 mile reach Crescent Nursery on the left and before the bridge over the B198, turn right. Path signed - Whitewebbs - and follow the farm drive towards Broadfield Farm. Approaching the farm, walk left around it, as path arrowed, and descend the track beyond. At the bottom bear slightly right to a stile and ascend to a stile and then along the righthand side of the field to another. Turn right and soon left to walk around the edge of Home Wood. In more than 1/4 mile gain a gate and shortly after Oldpark Ride (tarmaced).

Turn left with Theobalds Manor on your left. In a few yards turn right, as path signed - Whitewebbs - and walk beside the fence on your left. Reaching woodland, keep ahead beside it with the fence on your left to gain the footbridge over the M25. Cross over and descend the field to a footbridge. Keep ahead along the righthand side of the field to the next stile and onto another. Here follow a short hedged path right then left and continue along the righthand side of the field to pass Guy Lodge Stables on your left. Gain a stile and Whitewebbs Road, opposite the King & Tinker Inn. Turn right back to the car parking area.

FLASH LANE AQUEDUCT - It was built in 1820 at a cost of £252. 2 shillings. The cast iron trough is 18 feet wide, but this section of the New River was abandoned in 1850. The aqueduct was excavated in 1968.

WORMLEY WOOD AND GOFF'S OAK
- 6 MILES

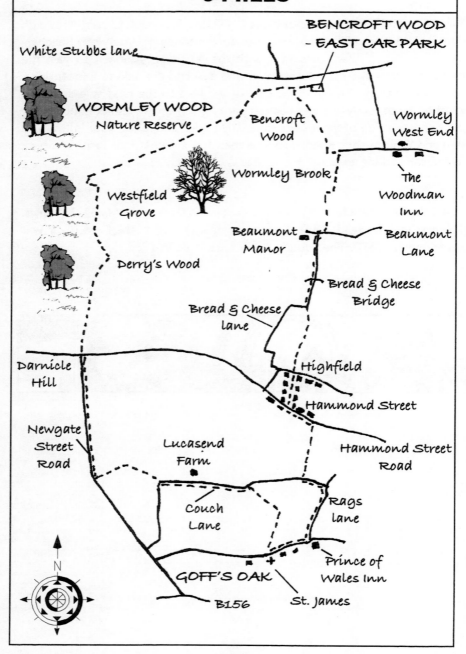

BENCROFT WOOD
- EAST CAR PARK

White Stubbs Lane

WORMLEY WOOD
Nature Reserve

Bencroft
Wood

Wormley
West End

Wormley Brook

The
Woodman
Inn

Westfield
Grove

Beaumont
Manor

Beaumont
Lane

Derry's Wood

Bread & Cheese
Bridge

Bread & Cheese
lane

Darnicle
Hill

Highfield

Hammond Street

Newgate
Street
Road

Lucasend
Farm

Hammond Street
Road

Couch
Lane

Rags
lane

N

Prince of
Wales Inn

GOFF'S OAK

B156

St. James

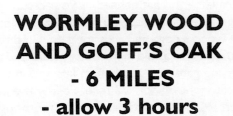

WORMLEY WOOD
AND GOFF'S OAK
- 6 MILES
- allow 3 hours

Basic route - Bencroft Wood East Car park - Bencroft Wood - Wormley Brook - Beaumont Road - Beaumont Manor - Bread & Cheese Lane - Bread & Cheese Bridge - Hammond Street - Burton Grange - Rags lane - Prince of Wales Inn - Goff's Oak - St. James Church - Crouch Lane - Newgate Street Road - Darnicle Hill - Derry's Wood - Westfield Grove - Wormley Wood - Bencroft Wood East Car Park.

Map - O.S. 1:25,000 Explorer Series No. 174 - Epping Forest & Lee Valley.

Car park and start - Bencroft Wood East Car Park; off White Stubbs Lane. Grid Ref. 174/331065.

Inns - The Woodman Inn, Wormley West End - 1/4 mile from route. The Prince of Wales Inn, Goff's Oak.

ABOUT THE WALK - You start in woodland before crossing rolling countryside, heading southwards to Hammond Street and onto Goff's Oak, where there is an inn. After crossing the Darnicle Hill road you return to woodland - Derry's Wood, Westfield Grove and Wormley Wood. Bencroft Wood is a National Nature Reserve, officially opened in June 1996 and is one of the most northern areas hornbeam oak. A surprising walk in delightful countryside on the western side of the Broxbourne District.

WALKING INSTRUCTIONS - Walk towards the car parks top lefthand corner and turn left onto a path with a marker post with red and purple bands. Follow the defined path for about five minutes, paralleling the road to

21

a pond and seat. Turn left - the path ahead is your return path - and follow the path which becomes track like as you walk through Bencroft Wood and in 1/4 mile reach the wood's edge and a kissing gate. Go through and keep to the lefthand side of the field to a stile in the bottom lefthand corner. Continue on the path to a kissing gate and road. Turn left and in a few yards right, footpath signed - Beaumont Manor 1/2 mile. Follow the paved path past a row of houses built in 1927. Beyond them cross a footbridge over Wormley Brook and ascend the field to a stile. Turn right and in a few yards left and keep the fence on your left to reach another stile and the Beaumont Road. turn right then left, passing Beaumont Manor high wall on your right, as you descend the Bread and Cheese Lane. Cross the Bread and Cheese Bridge over Turnford Brook, and ascend the road to where it turns sharp right. Here is a stile and path sign. Keep to the lefthand side of the field - hedge - to a footbridge and stiles and in 1/4 mile reach a stile and road on the edge of Hammond Street.

Turn left then right at Highfield, as path signed, and walk between the houses to Hammond Street Road. Turn left and in 1/4 mile opposite The Woodman Stores, turn right into Friern Close; path signed. Keep straight ahead on the path to Crouch Lane beside house no. 41. Turn left and in 100 yards right along the road to Rags lane. Follow this to Goff's Oak and the Prince of Wales Inn. Before it turn right along St. James Road. Immediately after the church - St. James - on the left, turn right as path signed and farm signed - Pylon Farm. Follow the farm track and pass Pylon Farm on the left. Continue on the track to a stile and on with the hedge on your right to a stile to your right. Turn half left and cross the field to the far top lefthand corner, following a faint path, to a stile. Continue to a footbridge and along the righthand side of the field to a stile and lane - Crouch lane. Turn right then left along the lane and pass Elm Farm on the left and later Lucasend Farm on the right. Where the lane turns sharp left turn right to a stile and path sign - Newgate Street Road. Follow the path half left across the field to the far top lefthand corner and a stile in a fence. Continue ahead in woodland and turn left on a fenced path and follow it to Newgate Street Road, beside path sign - Crouch Lane.

Turn right along Newgate Street Road, following the path on the left and in just over 1/2 mile reach the T junction with Darnicle Hill. Go straight across onto a tarmaced drive, path signed Brickendon. In 100 yards go through a gate and continue straight ahead on a path and in 1/4 mile reach another gate and Derry's Wood - Woodland Trust. Now on a track follow it right then left, now on a grass track through woodland bearing right to a footbridge. After keep to the lefthand path through Westfield Grove and in 1/4 mile the path turns left and soon right to a footbridge and seat. Cross and just after bear right onto a wide track through Wormley Wood, guided by wooden posts with a pink band. keep straight ahead on this track for 3/4 mile. In less than 1/2 mile cross a footbridge and later descend steps to another and ascend the other side to an Information Board and track. Turn left along the track and as you near the lane - White Stubbs Lane, turn right following the wooden posts with red and purple bands. Follow the path to the pond you passed at the start and keep ahead retracing your steps back to the car park.

GOFF'S OAK - Believed to be named after Sir Theodore Godfrey, who planted an oak tree here in 1066. The original oak tree could hold several people inside but blew down of February 2nd, 1950. St. James Church was started in 1860 and consecrated on St. James's Day, 25th. July 1862. St. James is the patron saint of Spain and many pilgrims follow the route to Santiago de Compostella, where his bones lie, in north-west Spain.

Scalloped shell, the symbol of a pilgrim, enroute to Santiago de Compostella, the resting place of St. James, the Patron saint of Spain. The Camino de St. Jacques is one of the major pilgrimage routes of the world, with more a million pilgrims walking a part of the route each year. The northern route across Spain is the most popular. Routes start from Le Puy, France; Seville, Spain - via la platta; and through Potugal from Lagos in the Algarve.

BROXBOURNE - Once a small village. The name is derived from the Saxon word Broc meaning badger; the path signs in the Broxbourne area include a badger symbol.

WORMLEY WEST END & BRICKENDON - 6 1/2 MILES

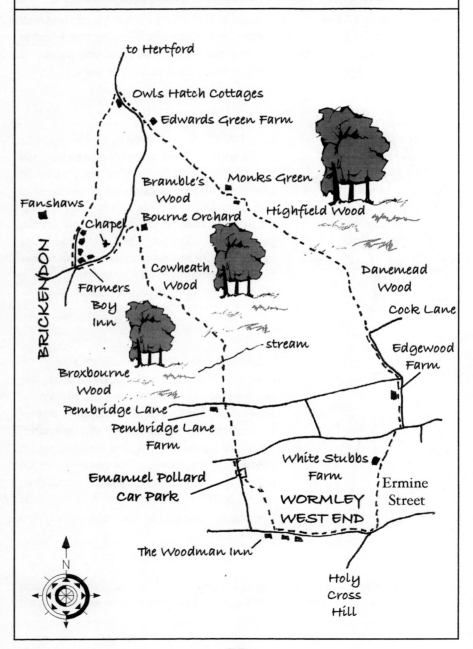

to Hertford

Owls Hatch Cottages

Edwards Green Farm

Bramble's Wood

Monks Green

Fanshaws

Chapel

Bourne Orchard

Highfield Wood

BRICKENDON

Cowheath Wood

Danemead Wood

Farmers Boy Inn

Cock Lane

Broxbourne Wood

stream

Edgewood Farm

Pembridge Lane

Pembridge Lane Farm

Emanuel Pollard Car Park

White Stubbs Farm

WORMLEY WEST END

Ermine Street

The Woodman Inn

Holy Cross Hill

N

WORMLEY WEST END & BRICKENDON
- 6 1/2 MILES
- allow 3 hours.

Basic route - Emanuel Pollard Car Park - White Stubbs Lane - Pembridge Lane Farm - Cowheath Wood - Bourne Orchard - Brickendon - Fanshaws Lane - Owls Hatch Cottages - Edwards Green farm - Monks Green - Bramble's Wood - Danesmead Wood - Edgewood Farm - White Stubbs Farm - Ermine Street - Wormley West End - Emanuel Pollard Car Park.

Map - O.S. 1:25,000 Explorer Series No. 174 - Epping Forest & Lee Valley.

Car Park and start - Emanuel Pollard Car park, just north of Wormley West End. Grid Ref. 174/335064.

Inns - The Farmers Boy, Brickendon. The Woodman, Wormley West End.

ABOUT THE WALK - A walk in the woods with the attractive village of Brickendon near the halfway point. This has a fine green, an inn and a fascinating small chapel, dedicated to Holy Cross and St. Albans. You return through more woodland and follow a small section of the Roman Road, Ermine Street. Finally, you walk through Wormley West End and just before the inn return to woodland and regain the car park.

WALKING INSTRUCTIONS - From the car park return to the road and turn right, ascending to the road junction - White Stubbs Lane. Cross to a kissing gate and the Hertfordshire Way. Keep ahead to two more kissing gates before bearing slightly left to stiles, passing a barn on the right and passing Pembridge Lane Farm on the left before Pembridge Lane.

Cross to a kissing gate, path signed Well Green 1 mile, and still on the Hertfordshire Way. Cross the field to another kissing gate and stables on the right. Now in a large field aim for the bottom righthand corner, where there is a footbridge and stile. Enter Cowheath Wood and follow the path right then left. A little later join a path from your right, keeping left along it as you walk through mixed woodlands. Pass a Barnes memorial seat and cross a track/fire break. Keep straight ahead on the path which becomes a wide one as you walk through pine trees to the wood's edge and a gate.

Keep the hedge/fence on your left for 1/4 mile to the house, Bourne Orchard, and a kissing gate and path sign - Pembridge lane 1 1/4 miles. Turn left on the permissive path and drive and pass Well Pond Cottage on your left, before reaching the Brickendon road. Turn left and soon pass the chapel dedicated to the Holy Cross and St. Albans on your right. Continue along the lane into Brickendon, passing the Five Horseshoes house on the right and the Farmers Boy Inn; just ahead is the Green. Immediately turn right along Fanshaws Lane passing houses on the right. Just after the lane to Fanshaws house turns left. Keep straight ahead on a track - a byway - and follow it northwards for 3/4 mile to the Brickendon Road and Owls Hatch Cottages on the right, built in 1900. Turn right on the Brickendon Road and in 200 yards pass Edwards Green Farm on the left and immediately afterwards turn left on a track, path signed Monks Green 1/2 mile. In less than 1/4 mile keep right to follow a smaller path/track which parallels the lane to Monks Green. Walk through and pass a row of barns on the right to reach a path junction.

Turn right, path signed Broxbourne Common 1 1/4 miles; bridlepath No. 14. The path/track soon turns left and keeps straight ahead through Bramble's Wood. After more than 1/2 mile (12 mins), cross a wet area with Danemead Wood Nature Reserve on the left - wooden walkways lead into the reserve on the left. Continue on the track and pass Bramble's Wood House on the right. Keep ahead to the road - Cock Lane. Follow it straight ahead passing Edgewood Farm on the right to the next junction with White Stubbs Lane. Turn right and a few yards left onto a track and pass White Stubbs Farm on the right. The track becomes a sunken one and follows the line of the Roman Road, Ermine Street. 1/2 mile from the road reach another - Holy Cross Hill - and turn right and right again, signed To Wormley West End.

Follow the road into the village and immediately before The Woodman Inn, turn right, as path signed - Stubbs Lane 1/2 mile. Keep the fence on the right to a stile and on up the lefthand side of the field to a kissing gate and woodland. Keep to the lefthand path to regain the Emanuel Pollard Car Park.

HERTFORDSHIRE WAY - 190 miles long circular walk within the county of Hertfordshire, starting and ending at Royston. Full details from the Friends of the Hertfordshire Way - www.fhw.org.uk

BRICKENDON - The manor for several centuries belonged to Waltham Abbey, and the monks worked the land, as the name Monk's Green reminds us. Brickendonbury House was built by the Clarke family in the early 18th. century. Later is passed to the Morgan family and they are responsible for the 3/4 mile long avenue of lime trees, known as Morgan's Walk. The parish is known as Brickendon Liberty for Henry 11 in 1184 gave the manor liberty from certain taxes.

The chapel, dedicated to the Holy Cross and St. Albans, was dedicated in 1932. The small building has pews from Ely Cathedral and the font was made from a sundial. In the churchyard is a Great Cross of oak, erected in 1931.

ERMINE STREET - Built in the first century AD, and ran from London via Lincoln to York. The name Ermine is believed to mean, *"The Street of the Eagle."*

WORMLEYBURY AND ERMINE STREET - 6 MILES

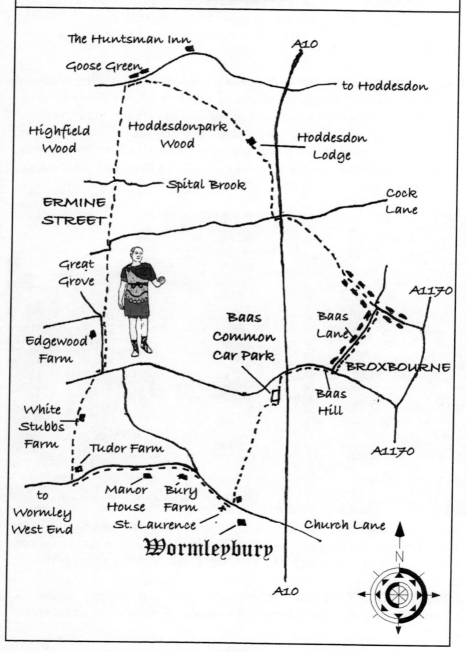

The Huntsman Inn

A10

Goose Green

to Hoddesdon

Highfield Wood

Hoddesdonpark Wood

Hoddesdon Lodge

Spital Brook

ERMINE STREET

Cock Lane

Great Grove

A1170

Edgewood Farm

Baas Common Car Park

Baas Lane

BROXBOURNE

White Stubbs Farm

Baas Hill

Tudor Farm

to Wormley West End

Manor House

Bury Farm

St. Laurence

Church Lane

A1170

𝔚𝔬𝔯𝔪𝔩𝔢𝔶𝔟𝔲𝔯𝔶

A10

N

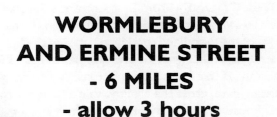

WORMLEBURY
AND ERMINE STREET
- 6 MILES
- allow 3 hours

Basic route - Baas Common Car Park - Church Lane, Wormleybury - Bury Farm - Manor House - Tudor Farm - Ermine Street - Edgewood Farm - Ermine Street - Great Grove - Danemead Wood - Spital Brook - Goose Green - Hoddesdonpark Wood - Hoddesdon Lodge - Cock Lane - Baas Lane (Hoddesdon) - Baas Hill - Baas Common Car Park.

Map - O.S. 1:25,000 Explorer Series No. 174 - Epping Forest & Lee Valley.

Car park and start - Baas Common, off Baas Hill. Grid Ref. 174/358067.
Alternative car parks beside Ermine Street at Martin Green and Goose Green.

Inn - Just off the route - 3 mins walk - at Goose Green, The Huntsman Inn.

ABOUT THE WALK - Baas Hill provides views southwards to the London skyline, before walking through a shallow vale to Wormleybury and its historic hall and church. Following quiet lanes you reach the line of the Roman Road - Ermine Street - and follow this northwards through woodland for more than 2 miles to Goose Green. A short distance off the route here is the Huntsman Inn, the only inn on the route. Next you cross Hoddesdonpark Wood to the wooden and attractive Hoddesdon Lodge. Afterwards you parallel the A10 before crossing it and walking through the western edge of Broxbourne to Baas Hill and car park. A delightfully varied walk.

WALKING INSTRUCTIONS - From Baas Common Car Park, walk to the end of the car park to a kissing gate and views to London. Turn right along the path along the edge of the woodland to a kissing gate on the left. Turn left and follow the path straight ahead, ignoring any side paths. Pass a footbridge to your right and keep ahead to a footbridge and trees. Walk through the narrow plantation to a kissing gate. cross the shallow vale aiming for the immediate right of a hedged house in the far righthand corner. Here gain a stile and follow the fenced path to Church Lane at Wormleybury. The impressive hall with a magnificent pillared portico can be seen through the trees just down to your left. Turn right and pass St. Laurence Church - well worth a visit - and follow the lane. Pass Bury Farm and keep left along the lane towards Wormley West End. Pass the Manor House on your left and 1/4 mile later Tudor Farm on the right.

Just after turn right onto a track, signed Ermine Street - the line of a former Roman Road. Follow the track slightly uphill and past the wooden houses of White Stubbs Farm to White Stubbs Lane. Turn right then left along Cock Lane, heading due north, and soon pass Edgewood Farm on your left. Just after the road divides into two and bears left. Keep right onto a track, still heading north, and now back on Ermine Street. Keep straight ahead along the track through woodland then through Great Grove to a lane. Go straight across and pass Ermine Street car park, at Martins Green on the right. Continue on the track passing Danemead Wood on the left - part of the Broxbourne Woods National Nature Reserve - scrub woodland and meadows rich in wildflowers. Later cross Spital Brook via footbridge on the left and ascend gently through Highfield Wood to Goose Green and car park. Here leave Ermine Street.

Turn right along the lane past the cottages of Goose Green and immediately after the last one on the left, turn right, as footpath signed and enter Hoddesdonpark Wood; managed by the Woodland Trust. If you walk a couple of minutes along the lane you come to the Huntsman Inn. There are many paths in this wood, but basically you keep straight ahead all the time, heading south-east to Hoddesdon Lodge, little over 1/2 mile away. First, soon cross a footbridge then cross a forest track. Continue ahead on the path/track which is signed periodically with yellow path arrows. Reach two wooden seats close together, after the second one keep right as yellow arrowed and continue through the wood on a track to a kissing gate on the wood's perimeter. Turn right, now on the Hertfordshire Way, and follow the track to the wooden Hoddesdon Lodge. Walk between the buildings to a kissing gate. Cross a field to a stile and on towards the embankment of the A10 to a kissing gate and path junction. Turn right and walk along the embankment slopes on a defined path to Cock Lane. Turn left and cross the A10 and pass a car park on the right.

Just after turn right to a kissing gate and path sign - still on the Hertfordshire Way. Walk beside a line of trees to a kissing gate and houses. Bear right to another kissing gate and walk through Park Lane Spinney to a kissing gate and path signs. Keep straight ahead and follow the fenced path, passing through two metal barriers at the start. Follow the path down to a road beside the house, Byron. Turn right then left and right again along Baas Lane. Follow it past the houses to Baas Hill road. Turn right and ascend gently and soon cross the A10 and immediately after turn left and regain Baas Common Car Park.

WORMLEYBURY - St. Laurence church - more than 900 years old and 1/2 mile from the main village; originally part of Waltham Abbey.

ERMINE STREET - Built in the first century AD, and ran from London via Lincoln to the Humber Estuary and onto York.

HODDESDONPARK WOOD - part of the Broxbourne Woods National Nature Reserve. One of the most northern areas for Hornbeam oak trees.

BAAS HILL - Takes its name from Henry de Baa, short for Bathonia, a Lord of the Manor in the 13th. century.

Hoddesdon Lodge.

31

GOOSE GREEN, ERMINE STREET AND HERTFORD HEATH - 6 MILES

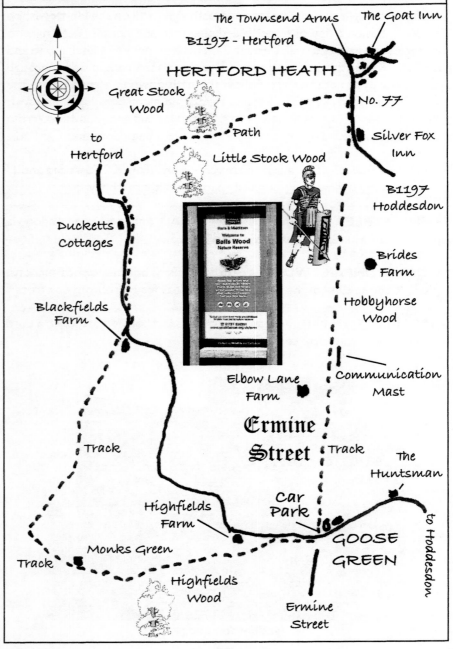

The Townsend Arms

The Goat Inn

B1197 - Hertford

HERTFORD HEATH

Great Stock Wood

No. 77

Path

to Hertford

Silver Fox Inn

Little Stock Wood

B1197 Hoddesdon

Ducketts Cottages

Brides Farm

Blackfields Farm

Hobbyhorse Wood

Communication Mast

Elbow Lane Farm

Ermine Street

Track

Track

The Huntsman

Highfields Farm

Car Park

Monks Green

GOOSE GREEN

to Hoddesdon

Track

Highfields Wood

Ermine Street

GOOSE GREEN, ERMINE STREET & HERTFORD HEATH
- 6 MILES
- allow 3 hours.

Basic route - Goose Green, Ermine Street Car Park - Elbow Lane/Ermine Street - Hobbyhorse Wood - Ermine Street - B1197 - Hertford Heath - Great Stock Wood - Little Stock Wood - Ducketts Cottages - Blackfields Farm - Monks Green - Highfields Wood - Mangrove Lane - Goose Green.

Map - O.S. 1:25,000 Explorer Series No. 174 - Epping Forest & Lee Valley.

Car park and start - Ermine Street Car Park at Goose Green. On Lord Street road from Hoddesdon. Grid Ref. 174/346088.

Inns - The Huntsman Inn, Goose Green - 3 mins from car park. Silver Fox Inn beside B1197 near Hertford Heath. The Goat Inn and The Townsend Arms, Hertford Heath, Green area.

ABOUT THE WALK - The route follows a two mile section of the Roman Road - Ermine Street, heading due north from Goose Green to Hertford Heath. The remainder of the walk is across fields and beside woodland, on good paths and tracks back to Goose Green. Whilst the route does not go into the "centre" of Hertford Heath, you are encouraged to visit the area and see the Green, inn and water fountain; a delightful little haven.

WALKING INSTRUCTIONS - From the car park gain the track - Ermine Street - and head due north along it. For the first part you have Elbow Lane on your left. After more than 1/2 mile pass Elbow Lane on your left and keep straight ahead passing the highest point in the area - 96m. - with a communication mast. Beyond pass Hobbyhorse Wood on your left with Balls

Wood beyond - Nature Reserve, officially opened on June 24th. 2009. Pass Brides Farm and Hertford Heath Nature Reserve, to your right and as you near the B1197 pass Ashleigh Paddocks. About 40 mins - 2 miles - from the car park reach the B1197 road with the Silver Fox Inn (named after a train), to your right.

Turn left along the road passing the Hertford Heath village sign on the right. Follow the road for 1/4 mile to house no. 77. Opposite is the path sign and your path, but first keep ahead to explore Hertford Heath. Pass a shop and Church Hill on your right - this is your return route. Keep ahead to the Townsend Arms and War Memorial. Turn right up Vicarage Causeway to The Green and Goat Inn. Turn right down Church Hill, passing the church and returning to the B1197 road. Turn left and at house no. 77, right to a kissing gate. Keep ahead on the defined path along the righthand side of the field - hedge. At the end turn right then left to continue now on a track to the perimeter of Great Stock Wood. As marked with path posts turn left then right, still on a track. Where the track turns left keep ahead with the wood on your right, as path signed, to a footbridge and path sign. Bear slightly left on the path to pass Little Stock Wood on your left. Keep straight ahead to a footbridge and turn left, as path signed, now on a track. Pass Kindle Warren Barns on your left and follow the now path with a hedge on your left to a stile, path sign and lane - Mangrove Lane.

Turn left along the lane and pass Ducketts Cottages on your right, then Peterfield Stables. Soon afterwards on your left is the drive to Freedom Farm. More than 1/4 mile later the road turns sharp left at Blackfields Farm. Turn right onto a track - Public Byway. Follow this for 1 1/4 miles to a track junction. Cross over and a few yards later left along another track, also a byway, to Monks Green, 1/4 mile away. Emerging at the farm and houses, keep straight ahead past them to a path junction. Keep ahead into a field - path signed - Highfields Farm 3/4 mile. Footpath No. 4. Keep to the righthand side of the field to gain a kissing gate in the far corner. Walk through Jepps Wood to another kissing gate. Continue ahead with Highfields Wood and fence on your right. Reach another kissing gate and continue close to the wood to a gate. Follow the fenced path left with farm buildings on the left. Continue right along the fenced path along the wood's edge with Highfields Farm to your left. Reach another kissing gate and bear half left and descend the field, along a fenced path, to a path sign and kissing gate, before reaching the other end of Mangrove Lane. Turn right and less than 1/4 mile later regain the car park at Goose Green on your left. 3 mins ahead along the lane brings you to the Huntsman Inn.

HERTFORD HEATH - Lies on the Roman Road - Ermine Street - the route taken to Hertford Castle by the Kings and Queens from London during the Plague. On the Green is the village well but by 1897 this was considered unfit. The vicar had a well sunk in his garden and a fountain by the village well, for the children. In the late 19th. century the villagers did washing for the surrounding mansions and they all had a specific area of the Green to hang out the washing to dry.

The village sign shows places around the Green with Haileybury College at the bottom.

Ermine Street.

RYE HOUSE, NEW RIVER & HAILEYBURY - 8 MILES

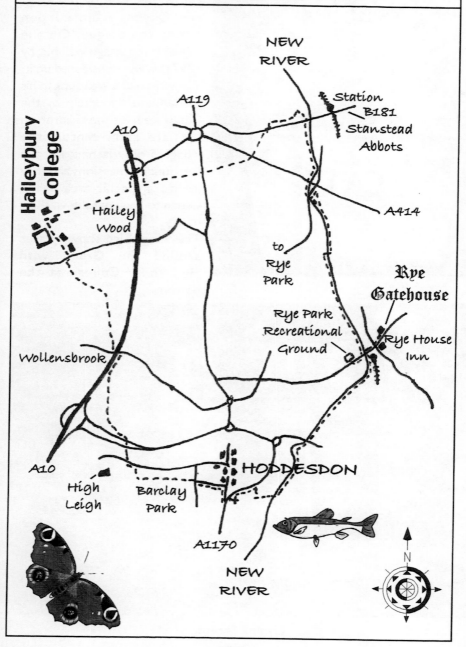

NEW RIVER

A119

Station
B181
Stanstead
Abbots

A10

Haileybury College

Hailey Wood

A414

to Rye Park

Rye Gatehouse

Rye Park Recreational Ground

Rye House Inn

Wollensbrook

HODDESDON

High Leigh

Barclay Park

A1170

NEW RIVER

N

RYE HOUSE, NEW RIVER & HAILEYBURY
- 8 MILES
- allow 3 to 4 hours

Basic route - Rye House Gatehouse Car Park - New River - A414 - B181, St. Margarets - A414 - A1170 - A10 - Hailey Wood - Haileybury - Dells Wood - Wollensbrook - B1197 - High Leigh - Barclay Park - Hoddesdon - New River - Rye House Gatehouse.

Map - O.S. 1:25,000 Explorer Series No. 174 - Epping Forest & Lee Valley.

Car Park and start - Rye House Gatehouse Car Park, east of Rye House Station. Alternative on the west side - Rye Park Recreational Ground.

Inns - Rye House Inn. Several in Hoddesdon.

Cafe - Several in Hoddesdon.

ABOUT THE WALK - Whilst the route is bisected by several roads, including the A10, don't let this put you off! The walk is a delight and full of surprises. First along a remote and unspoilt section of the New River to the Stanstead Abbots road (B181). Next you cross several roads on good paths before walking into Haileybury College. Here on a right of way you walk through the college campus, past its impressive buildings. Onward you cross fields to Wollensbrook and beside Barclay Park to central Hoddesdon; here are inns and cafe's. Beyond you rejoin the New River and follow it along a most picturesque section back to Rye House. There are two car parks here, basically on either side of the New River and River Lee Navigation. I chose the Rye Gatehouse car park for the gatehouse and moated grounds are full of interest and worth exploring. You can do it as a circular walk using the train at Rye House Station.

WALKING INSTRUCTIONS - From Rye Gatehouse car park, return along the road or past the gatehouse to the Rye House Inn and across the River Lee Navigation. Pass the Rye House Station and turn right onto the New River path; on the opposite side of the road is your return path by the river. Keep the river on your right for more than 1/2 mile to a bridge with Cranbourne Level Crossing down to your right. Cross the bridge and turn left at the kissing gate and continue beside the river, now on your left. Shortly reach the St. Margarets Community Woods and leave the riverside. Keep to the righthand path which takes through woodland to the Hoddesdon road and A414 flyover. Turn left and pass the Rye Common Water Treatment Plant on your right. Just after cross a bridge over the New River and turn right to walk beside the New River; now on your right. Follow it for nearly 1/2 mile along a delightful stretch of the river to the B181 road.

Go straight across and in a few yards keep left to walk past the single storey houses of Folly View Nos. 26/34. At the end turn left along the aptly named New River Avenue to its junction. Turn left to the B181 road. Cross to your right to the path sign - Path No. 1 - Ware Road 1/2 mile. Follow the defined path to a bridge over the A414 and onto the A1170, Ware Road. Go straight across to a path sign and stile. Keep beside the fence on your left to a barn and stile. Continue straight ahead along the lefthand side of the field to the field corner and stile. Follow the path right and down, as signed, to the A10 slip road. bear left and walk through the underpass and turn left, as path signed, up a path above a slip road; footpath signed - Hertford Heath 1 mile. At the top turn right and follow the grass path on the right of Hailey Wood. Keep straight ahead along the path to a footpath sign. The path now becomes a track as you head towards Haileybury College; on the right are playing fields. Walk right up to the buildings with the Sports Complex on your right. Turn left between the buildings, passing the Cricket field on your left, then as you follow the drive, pass the Bradby Hall on your left and later the Science building. Behind you can see the impressive Terrace building.

Gaining the road turn right then left at a stile by a path sign, with the Tennis courts on your left. Follow the faint path past the courts and on down to the far side the field - hedge. Bear left beside it on your right and follow it to its far corner and second kissing gate on the right. Cross to a stile and keep the hedge on your left to a kissing gate and then the fence on your right before descending and curving round in woodland to the road at Woollensbrook. Turn left and pass under the A10 and immediately right onto a fenced path. Follow the defined path right up the slope near the A10 road, before it turns left on a hedged path. This later becomes a track and turns left then right to pass through two underpasses beneath the A10 slip roads from Hoddesdon. Continue straight ahead beyond along the concrete track to the road, Lord Street. To your right is the entrance to High Leigh Conference Centre.

Turn left and in a few yards right, as path signed, and follow the path past houses on the left. Follow the path round to your left and now a tarmaced path as you walk beside Barclay Park on your right. Later pass the Hoddesdon Lawn Tennis Club. Keep straight ahead to the road. Cross to your right and follow Brocket Road all the way to the pedestrianised shopping area of Hoddesdon. As you enter and to your left are cafe and inns. Turn right to the A1170 road. Cross and turn left past St. Augustine's Catholic Church. After a short distance pass the Jehovah Witness church and turn right into Lampits and left into Rivermead. On the righthand side is the path sign and path; follow this to the New River. Cross the bridge and turn left keeping the river on your left. Soon cross Conduit Lane and continue by the river to a road in 1/4 mile. Cross using the kissing gates and continue by the river on your left. In almost 1/2 mile bear right to the kissing gate and left then right to continue by the river. In 1/4 mile reach the road with Rye House Station on your right, where you began. Turn right and cross the River Lee Navigation and pass the Rye House Inn and on to the Gatehouse and car park.

HAILEYBURY COLLEGE - Celebrated its 100th. anniversary in 1962, which was celebrated by a visit by H.M. Queen Elizabeth IInd., as a memorial plaque on a school building, which you pass as you walk through. The college began in 1862 from an existing college for Civil Servants of the East India Company. The fine classical Terrace and dome was designed by William Wilkins, who also designed the National Gallery.

BARCLAY PARK - Originally part of High Leigh estate bought in 1871 by Robert Barclay. Following his death in 1921, High Leigh became a Conference Centre and much of the park was given for public use by family.

HODDESDON - The town centre is a conservation area with several listed buildings, including the 17th. century inns - The Swan and The Salisbury Arms. The Clock Tower was built in 1835 and is on the site of a chapel, dedicated to St. Katherine, built in 1336. Inside is a chapel bell dated 1510.

RIVER LEE NAVIGATION AND NEW RIVER - 10 MILES

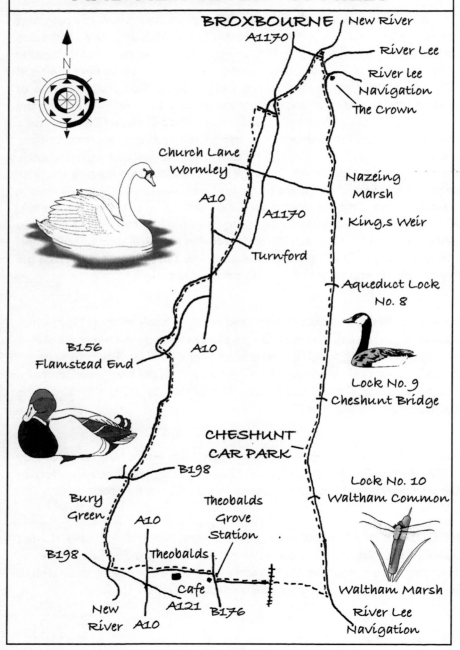

BROXBOURNE — New River

A1170

River Lee

River lee Navigation

The Crown

Church Lane Wormley

Nazeing Marsh

A10

A1170

King,s Weir

Turnford

Aqueduct Lock No. 8

B156 Flamstead End

A10

Lock No. 9 Cheshunt Bridge

CHESHUNT CAR PARK

B198

Lock No. 10 Waltham Common

Bury Green

Theobalds Grove Station

A10

Theobalds

B198

New River

Cafe

A121 B176

A10

Waltham Marsh

River Lee Navigation

RIVER LEE NAVIGATION AND NEW RIVER
- 10 MILES
- allow 4 hours

Basic route - Car Park near Cheshunt Station - River Lee Navigation - Lock No. 9 - Lock No. 8, Aqueduct Lock - Broxbourne Car Park - New River - Wormley - Turnford - Flamstead End - Bury Green - New River - A10 - Theobalds (Cedar Park) - Theobalds Grove Station - Marsh Bridge - River Lee Navigation - Lock No. 10, Waltham Common Lock - Cheshunt Car Park.

Map - O.S. 1:25,000 Explorer Series No. 174 - Epping Forest & Lee Valley.

Car park and start - Beyond Cheshunt Station, beside the River Lee Navigation. Reached down the road from the B176 in Cheshunt, signed Station and YHA - Pindar Car park - Grid Ref. 174/369024. Alternative start and car park, Broxbourne, between the River Lee Navigation and New River; Grid Ref. 174/372068. The walk can be started using the train at Theobalds Grove Station.

Inns - The Crown, Broxbourne, just off the route beside the River Lee Navigation; nearly halfway point of the route. The Wheatsheaf Inn, Theobalds Grove Station.

Cafe - Broxbourne Car park; seasonal. Theobalds; Cedar Park Tea Room.

ABOUT THE WALK - A spectacular river/canal walk combining both the River Lee Navigation and New River. They provide a delightful contrast from the "busy" canal to the peaceful New River. Both team with Mute Swans, Canada Geese, Mallards, Coots and Moorhens. I choose to start the walk from near Cheshunt Station but there are several other car parks beside the

River Lee Navigation. An alternative start could be from Broxbourne. Like a fine wine it is not to be hurried, but an enjoyable riverside wander in Hertfordshire; both the creation of man in the 17th and 18th. centuries.

WALKING INSTRUCTIONS - Starting from Cheshunt (Pindar) Car Park, gain the River Lee Navigation and turn left along it - path signed, Broxbourne - keeping the canal on your right. In 1/2 mile pass Lock No. 9 - Cheshunt Lock. In another mile pass Lock No. 8 - Aqueduct Lock. Keep beside the canal for another two miles to Broxbourne, turning left up a side channel before a bridge, to Broxbourne car park. At the junction, just over the bridge and another one is The Crown - inn and restaurant. In the car park is a seasonal refreshment van.

Follow the car park road out of the car park to Mill Lane. Turn left along it and in 100 yards left to walk along the tarmaced lane beside the New River. The New River path signs guide you for the next five miles. Pass allotments on your left and after nearly 1/2 mile go through a kissing gate; a feature of the New River Path, and gain the A1170 road. The next section of the New River has no path. Turn left and 50 yards later right, as path signed, along Lozeno Lane. Follow it past the houses and across the New River and a little further ahead turn left on a path along the lefthand side of the field. Gain a kissing gate and keep left on the path back to the New River; which is now on your left. Follow it to Church Lane, Wormley. Go basically straight across to continue beside the New River. 1/2 mile later pass under road at Turnford and then as you near the A10 cross to the lefthand side of the river and continue with it on your right. Pass under the A10 and continue beside the river on your right for nearly 3/4 mile to the road near Flamstead End - B156.

Cross using the kissing gates and continue on the concrete pathway with the earth embankment of a reservoir on your right. Follow the path to another kissing gate and road in Cheshunt. Cross over to continue beside the New River and 300 yards later cross a bridge over the river and turn left. Continue now with the river on your left for almost a mile. Pass Bury Green and as you near the B198 road, cross another footbridge over the river and continue with it on your right. Before the road and underpass, turn left through a stile and follow a broken fence path to a track. Turn left along it past a thatched house to the A10 road. The central crash barrier been divided to act as a path. Cross with care to the barrier and turn right for a few yards before crossing the other carriageway to Theobalds Lane. Follow the lane past Cedar Park, where there is a tea-room/cafe. Follow the road straight ahead past the houses to the B176 and Theobalds Grove Station on the right.

Turn right then left opposite the Wheatsheaf Inn along Trinity Lane. Follow it past the houses and cross the railway line into the River Lee Country Park. Follow the path over a bridge and right to the River Lee Navigation. Turn left and walk beside the navigation for a mile. In more than 1/2 mile pass Lock No. 10 - Waltham Common. Little over 1/4 mile later on a bend in the navigation leave it on the left to regain Cheshunt (Pindar) car park, where you began a few hours ago.

RIVER LEE NAVIGATION - Length - Limehouse Basin, Bow to Hertford - 27 3/4 miles. 19 locks.

The River Lee has been, since Roman times, an important trade route to London. An Act of 1571 for an artificial cut was made to help speed up the traffic. At the same time a pound at Waltham Abbey with lock gates - a similar principal to today - was made and is one of the earliest in the country. During the 18th and 19th. century the navigation was improved, these included in 1769 the Waltham, Edmonton and Hackney Cuts (avoiding the River Lee) and pound locks was opened. In 1911 The Lee Conservancy bought the River Stort Navigation and improved it together with the River Lee. By 1930, 130 ton boats could reach Enfield and 100 ton boats to Ware and Hertford. During the rest of the 20th. century many improvements were made including mechanised locks. Whilst many of the locks vary in size the majority are - 85 ft long by 16 ft wide and between 5 and 7 feet deep. Upto Enfield Lock they are double locks and beyond to Hertford, single locks. The river can be either spelt Lee or Lea.

CEDAR PARK - The park is the site of the Royal Palace of Theobalds, originally built about 1563 by Lord Burleigh, Secretary of State, Lord High Treasurer and Master of Requests to Queen Elizabeth Ist; who often visited here. Upon Lord Burleigh death in 1598, his son, Sir Robert Cecil (became the first Earl of Salisbury and the King's first Minister) took over and in 1603, he entertained James the First here. The king liked Theobalds and swapped it for Hatfield House in 1607; thereby becoming a Royal Palace. It was here that James Ist. died in 1625 and Charles Ist. who had been brought up here, became King. Later Charles Ist. rode from here to Nottingham and raised his standard at the Civil War. He later lost to the Parliamentarians and was executed. His property was seized and ransacked and sold off. By 1783 the property was described "as ruinous". In 1920 the area was given to the Cheshunt Council. The main entrance gates, which you pass, has plaques and coats of arms on showing its history. over the last 450 years. The park is most attractive and part of the ruins can still be seen; there is also a cafe. Hatfield House is still owned today by the Cecil family and is a particularly fine Jacobean House. Queen Elizabeth the First was brought up here.

For nearly a century the Temple Bar gate stood in the grounds, being bought by Sir Henry Meux, a wealthy brewer and a former owner of Theobalds. The Temple Bar Inn in Cheshunt still recalls its name. In 2004 it was removed and rebuilt beside St. Paul's Cathedral, being the last remaining 17th. century (1672) gate into the city

BRICKENDON, BAYFORD & HERTFORD - 8 MILES

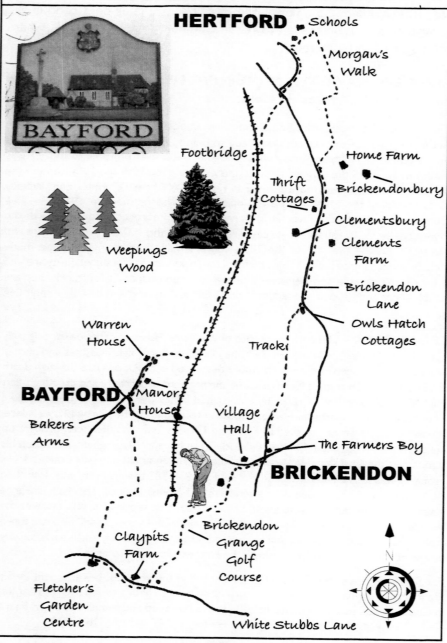

HERTFORD

Schools

Morgan's Walk

Footbridge

BAYFORD

Thrift Cottages

Home Farm

Brickendonbury

Clementsbury

Clements Farm

Brickendon Lane

Owls Hatch Cottages

Weepings Wood

Warren House

Track

Manor House

BAYFORD

Bakers Arms

Village Hall

The Farmers Boy

BRICKENDON

Claypits Farm

Brickendon Grange Golf Course

Fletcher's Garden Centre

White Stubbs Lane

N

44

BRICKENDON, BAYFORD
& HERTFORD
- 8 MILES
- allow 3 1/2 hours.

Basic route - Brickendon - Brickendon Grange Golf Course - Ponsbourne Tunnel - White Stubbs Lane - Claypits Farm - Fletcher Garden Centre - Bayford - Manor House - Hertfordshire Way - Brickendon Lane - Hertford - Morgan's Walk - Brickendon Lane - Brickendon.

Map - O.S. 1:25,000 Explorer Series No. 174 - Epping Forest and Lee Valley.

Car Park and start - Beside The Green, Brickendon.

Inns - The Farmers Boy, Brickendon. Bakers Arms, Bayford.

Ice Cream - Fletchers Garden Centre, White Stubbs Lane.

ABOUT THE WALK - A quiet and peaceful route along paths and tracks, passing through the interesting and unspoilt villages of Brickendon and Bayford. From Bayford you join the Hertfordshire Way and follow it to the fringe of Hertford. Here you turn south to return to Brickendon and its Green.

WALKING INSTRUCTIONS - Starting from The Green, with The Farmers Boy Inn on the right - you return to here at the end - follow the road left to Bayford, passing the Green on your left. Pass the Village Hall on the right with a car park opposite. Just after turn left at the Poplars, footpath signed - White Stubbs Lane 1 mile. Follow the drive into the Brickendon Grange Golf Course,

45

with The Grange on the right. Walk through the car park to its lefthand corner. The whole right of way through the golf course is marked with blue posts and occasional white arrows on the trees. First follow it straight ahead past the 13th hole before turning right passing the 10th hole, and onto the righthand side of the course. Take care crossing the fairways and observe what the golfers are doing! Follow the posts left beside the wood on the right, eventually reaching a stile and end of the golf club area. Continue with the wood - Blackfan Wood - on the right to the next stile and on along a defined path to White Stubbs Lane and stile; to your left is an air shaft of the Ponsbourne Tunnel. The footpath sign at the lane says it is 1 1/4 miles to Brickendon!

Turn right along the lane passing Claypits Farm. 1/4 mile later opposite the Fletchers Garden Centre, turn right onto a wooded track, signed - Public Byway No. 8 - Bayford 1 mile. Follow the track northwards, around the edge of Blackfan Wood and 1/2 mile reach Keepers Cottage on the right. Here the track turns sharp left and follow it all the way to Bayford. Reaching the road turn left to the village centre with the Bakers Arms on the left. Turn right into a lane, path signed - Herford 2 1/2 miles; you are now on a section of the Hertfordshire Way. Pass the Old School, then Manor House on the right and Warren House on the left. Just after is Walnut Cottage. Continue on the track and before you approach the last house, turn right, as path signed and stiled. Keep beside the hedge on your left to a stile, then beside a fence on your left to a thicket and stile. Turn left and now walk along the edge of a large field with the railway line to your right. In 1/2 mile turn right then left over a footbridge and continue in woodland close to the railway line. Cross another footbridge and in 1/4 mile pass some large pine trees. 1/4 mile later walk along a fenced path to the footbridge over the railway line. Cross and moments later the path divides. Keep left along the field edge and follow the path by the hedge, with houses beyond, for 1/4 mile to Brickendon Lane, on the edge of Hertford.

Turn left then right and ascend Mandeville Road - Herts. Way signed. Follow the curving road round to your left and in 1/4 mile before the road descends, turn right into Wilton Crescent - Herts. Way signed - and right again onto a tarmaced path. Pass a school on your left and playing fields on the right, as the path becomes a hedged path. Emerge onto a road. To your left the centre of Hertford is 1/2 mile away. Leave the Herts. Way and turn right onto a path; not the road, and soon gain the path along Morgan's Walk - lime tree avenue. A 1/3 mile along here (7/8 mins), turn right at the footpath post (bridleway) and walk into the field to a path sign. Turn left to a field gap and continue with the hedge on your left, following a defined path. This leads

46

to a gate and beyond bear slightly right and ascend the slope on the path before descending to a footbridge and Brickendon Lane.

Turn left along the lane and follow it for 3/4 mile (15 mins). First pass the entrance to Brickendonbury on your left, with lodge dated 1896, on the left. Soon after on the right Thrift Cottages, then Clementsbury and on the left Clements Farm. 1/4 mile later the road turns left with Owl Hatch Cottages and four tall pine trees. Just before them turn right onto a track. Follow the wooded track for a mile and in its later stages a water treatment plant on the left before gaining Fanshaws lane. Follow it past the houses to the road beside The Farmers Boy Inn in Brickendon. To your right is The Green.

BAYFORD - In 1757 the Manor was sold to Sir William Baker M.P. He built the nearby Bayfordbury house and his descendants lived here for some 200 years. They rebuilt the church in 1871 and the Baker Vault lies in the churchyard. Their name and arms are preserved in the local inn/hotel.

BRICKENDON - The manor for several centuries belonged to Waltham Abbey, and the monks worked the land, as the name Monk's Green reminds us. Brickendonbury House was built by the Clarke family in the early 18th. century. Later is passed to the Morgan family and they are responsible for the 3/4 mile long avenue of lime trees, known as Morgan's Walk. The parish is known as Brickendon Liberty for Henry 11 in 1184 gave the manor liberty from certain taxes.

Farmers Boy Inn and The Five Horseshoes, Brickendon.
47

HERTFORD HEATH, GREAT AMWELL AND NEW RIVER - 8 MILES

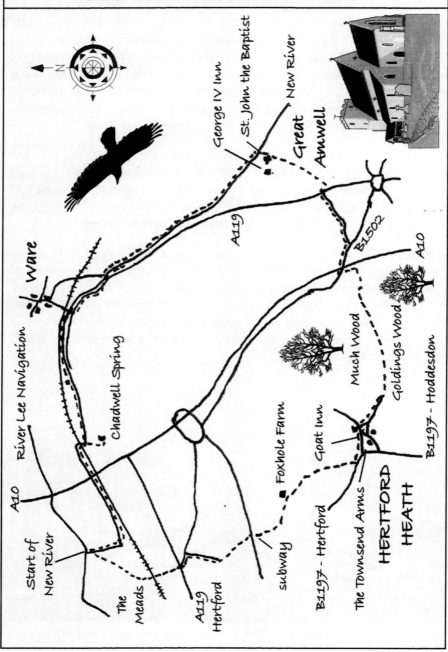

48

HERTFORD HEATH, GREAT AMWELL AND NEW RIVER
- 8 MILES
- allow 3 1/2 hours.

Basic route - Hertford Heath - Goldings Wood & Much Wood - B1502 - Great Amwell - New River - Ware - Chadwell Spring - King's Mead - River Lee Navigation - The Meads - A119 - Hertford - Foxhole Farm - Hertford Heath.

Map - O.S. 1:25,000 Explorer Series No. 174 - Epping Forest and Lee Valley.

Car Park and start - The Green, opposite The Goat Inn in Hertford Heath. Roadside parking only.

Inns - The Townsend Arms and The Goat Inn, Hertford Heath. George IV Inn, Great Amwell, just off the route. The John Gilpin, and Royal Oak Inn, Ware - several others off the route in central Ware.

Cafe - In Central Ware, just off the route.

ABOUT THE WALK - Probably the best walk in the book! Starting from Hertford Heath you walk through stunning woodland - Hertford Heath Nature Reserve (Goldings Wood and Much Wood) - to the A10. passing under it you follow a lane and path to the remarkable haven of Great Amwell, around the church of St. John the Baptist and New River Pond. Plaques here recall the origins of the New River, which you now follow for 2 1/2 miles to its junction with the River Lee Navigation. A short side path takes you to Chadwell Spring, the original source of the New River in 1613. Heading southwards you pass through the suburb of Hertford before ascending fields back to

Hertford Heath and its pleasant Green. Certainly a walk to savour!

WALKING INSTRUCTIONS - Starting from The Green in Hertford Heath, take the No Through Road opposite the Goat Inn, heading eastwards. Pass the Old School and follow the lane to its end at house no. 69 on the left. Here gain the bridleway path and enter the Hertford Heath Nature Reserve. In a few yards keep to the lefthand track and follow this through woodland which becomes almost a ceremonial track way, lined with overhanging trees. In less than 1/2 mile pass a farm as the track turns right then left and on down a fenced path to the embankment of the A10. Turn left, as path signed, to the B1502 road and A10 underpass. Turn right and walk through and in 100 yards, opposite the house, Little Thele, turn left along Gypsy Lane. Follow it for 1/4 mile to A119 road. Turn right and in a few yards left at the footpath sign. Follow the defined path by the hedge to a kissing gate. Continue straight ahead on a lane and pass Glebe House (1864) on the right and Walton Lodge on the left. Immediately afterwards bear left on the signed path and descend to St. John the Baptist Church in Great Amwell, passing its Norman Apse end. To explore the church turn left and beyond the main gate is the George IV Inn.

Descend the steps by the church end to reach the New River and turn left. The pond here has plaques detailing the New River; one stating that Chadwell Spring, where it began in 1613 is two miles away - a side path later takes you there. The end stone epitaph has the following poem by Nares, 1818, on it -

> Well, perpetual be thy Stream
> Nor 'eer thy spring be lefs
> Which thousands drink who never dream
> whence flows the boon they bless.
>
> To often thus ungrateful man
> Blind this unconscious lives,
> Enjoys kind heav'ns indulgent plan,
> Nor thinks of him who gives.

Cross the road to a kissing gate and walk beside the New River on your left; it is now your companion for the next 2 1/2 miles. In 1/2 mile using kissing gates cross a minor road and continue with the river on your left and the A119 - London Road - beyond. In another 1/2 mile gain the road and turn left then right to walk along London Road, with the New River on your right. At the road is the John Gilpin Inn. Pass the Royal Oak Inn and at the next road into Ware - Amwell End - turn right then left onto the path beside the New River. Just down the road is central Ware with all amenities - shops, inns, cafe etc., In little over 1/4 mile pass Broadmeadows Pumping Station on your right, with a tall chimney. Continue with the river on your left and in another 1/4 mile the river turns right at the White Sluice House and Marble Gauge Station dated 1770. Here a path on your left leads along an embankment between "lakes". At the end turn left to reach the fence surrounding Chadwell Spring, where the New River began in 1613 - 40 miles to London. The stone monument here records the details.

Retrace your steps back to the New River. On the opposite side can be seen a stone marker - *"This belongs to New River Company, South Ward."* Continue along the path beside the New River; now with it on your right and cross the railway line and follow the path left. In 1/2 mile turn right across a footbridge over the river and head for the New Gauge Station on the River Lee Navigation, built in 1856. Just before it on your left is another bridge and your next path. But first it is worth seeing the Navigation and the plaque of the start of the New River path. The gauge here is where the River Lee is taken into the New River to boost the imput from Chadwell Spring.

Return a few yards to the bridge and cross and bear left along the gravel path across The Meads, a Nature Reserve, which are the largest grazed riverside flood meadows in Hertfordshire. Cross to a kissing gate and onto the railway line and continue ahead, now along Rowley Road to the A119 road. At the road cross to your half left to follow Stanstead Road. In a few yards take the second road on your right - Foxhole Avenue, a No Through Road, and follow it to where it turns right at house no. 65. Keep ahead to a gate and children's play area. Follow the wooded path and where it forks keep to the righthand path which leads to a subway in the A414 road. Walk through and continue ahead to a stile. Bear left to another and onto a drive. Turn left to Foxholes Farm and keep to its righthand side, as path signed to a kissing gate. Keep to the lefthand side of the field - hedge - and follow it right and up. In less than 1/2 mile reach the B1197 road. Turn left and left again into Vicarage Causeway, passing the Hertford Heath War Memorial on your right and The Townsend Arms beyond. Ascend to The Goat Inn and the Green.

HERTFORD HEATH - Lies on the Roman Road - Ermine Street - the route taken to Hertford Castle by the Kings and Queens from London. On the Green is the village well but by 1897 this was considered unfit. The vicar had a well sunk in his garden and a fountain by the village well, for the children. In the late 19th. century the villagers did washing for the surrounding mansions and they all had a specific area of the Green to hang out the washing to dry.

GREAT AMWELL - Below the church is the New River Pond with several monuments. Sir Hugh Myddleton, a Welsh engineer, who in 1609 - 1613 began the New River to take clear water from Chadwell Spring to Clerkenwell, London. At first it was 40 miles long but today only 23 miles remain and is still used by Thames Water Board; the river is also fed by the River Lee.

WARE - The Priory was once occupied in the 14th. century by Franciscan Monks. Founded by Thomas Wake, the Lord of the Manor in 1338. St. Mary the Virgin has a 14th. century octagonal font, and is considered one of the finest in Hertfordshire. The name Chauncy recalls Sir Henry Chauncy who presided over one the last witch trails in England. Jane Wenham was sentenced to death but was reprieved by Queen Anne; this led to the abolishment of witchcraft laws in England.

The Goat Inn and Water Fountain, Hertford Heath.

The New River - a gem in surburbia.

West Reservoir and Stoke Newington.

NEW RIVER - A10 to Islington - 16 miles

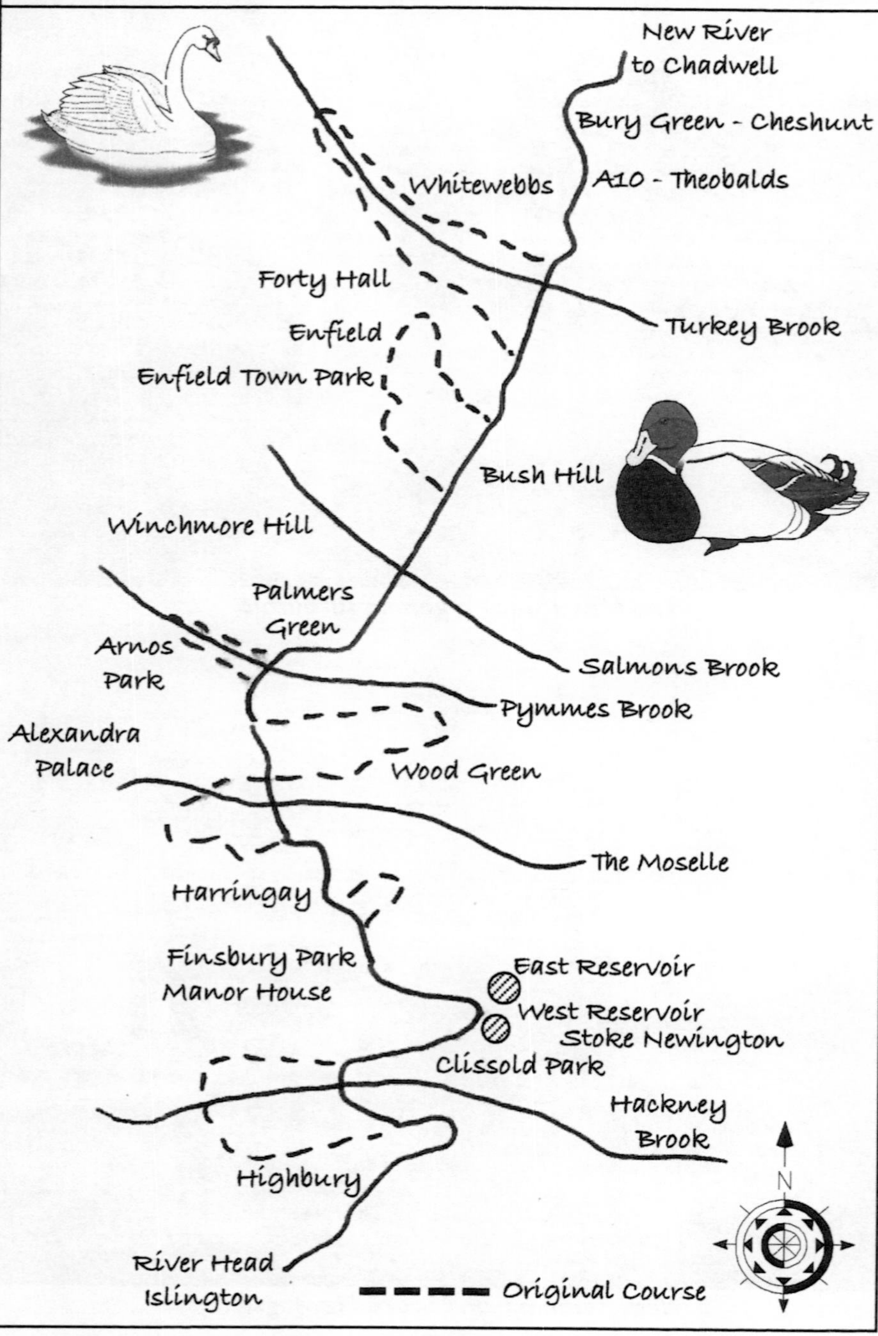

New River
to Chadwell

Bury Green - Cheshunt

Whitewebbs

A10 - Theobalds

Forty Hall

Enfield

Turkey Brook

Enfield Town Park

Bush Hill

Winchmore Hill

Palmers
Green

Arnos
Park

Salmons Brook

Pymmes Brook

Alexandra
Palace

Wood Green

The Moselle

Harringay

Finsbury Park
Manor House

East Reservoir

West Reservoir
Stoke Newington

Clissold Park

Hackney
Brook

Highbury

River Head
Islington

N

- - - - Original Course

NEW RIVER
- A10/M25 to River Head, Islington
- 16 miles
- allow 6 to 7 hours.

Basic route - Bullsmoor Lane - beside A10 - Forty Hill - Enfield - Enfield Town Park - Bush Hill - Winchmore Hill - Palmers Green - Alexandra Palace - Hornsey - Harringay - Finsbury Park - East and West Reservoirs - Clissold park - Highbury - Islington.

Map - O.S. 1:25,000 Explorer Series No. 173 - London North.

Start - Junction of Bullsmoor Lane and A10, near Junction 25 of M25. Reached by bus no. 217.

End - Islington with The Angel Underground Station, closeby.

Inns - Numerous close to the route.

ABOUT THE WALK - For a long while I felt I had not done justice to the New River, as I had not walked it from the Forty Hall area, south to London. The whole walk - end to end - from Chadwell to London is 24 miles, and well signed. The section described here, follows a narrow strip of waterway paradise through London suburbia to the River Head at Islington, close to the Sadlers Wells theatre. It is a delightful walk, much of the time you are beside the river and where it now runs through tunnels or pipes, you road walk either above it or along the nearest road to it. As you pass many tube stations and bus routes, you can either walk it one go, as I did, or do it in stages at your own pace. I have not gone into great detail as to the walking instructions, for the route is well signed with green - New River Path - signs. Plus at frequent intervals there is a historical board detailing each section with a map and some brief history. There are many attractive places on the way, such as Enfield Town Park, Finsbury Park, the East and West Reservoirs, and Clissold Park. The final section along Colebrook Row, is particularly attractive, despite the river being underground, you walk through limestone bouldered parks, before walking past Sadlers Wells theatre to the River's Head viewing platform. This site has history boards and the former head pond is now marked out with a small fountain in the middle. Before returning home it is appropriate to walk along Islington High Street, just past the Angel Inn and close to the Camden Antique Market, to see the impressive statue to Sir Hugh Myddleton.

BRIEF WALKING INSTRUCTIONS - I started at the Bullsmoor Lane junction with the A10, before Junction 25 of the M25 - Grid Ref. 348997. A short distance up Bullsmoor Lane - westwards - you reach the New River. Turn left onto the path and keep beside the river for 1/2 mile to an automatic weed/rubbish extracting overhead crane. The path now keeps left to keep near a fence on your right; to your right is the old course of the river through Whitewebbs. At the London Loop cross path turn right then left to continue by the river past Carterhatch Lane and onto Enfield and the A110 road. Here you bear right towards Enfield Town picking up a water filled section of the Enfield Loop River. Approaching the main shopping area you turn right to the Civic Centre and left into parkland to follow the loop round to your left to the opposite end of the shopping area and bus station. Cross the road and continue in Enfield Town Park, by the river loop.

In more than five minutes bear right across the river to gain Carr Lane, following it left past Bush Hill Golf Course on the right, to a road. Keep straight ahead along the road and right over Salmon Brook and beside the New River for a short section. Continue through Winchmore Hill and onto Palmers Green and cross the Pymmes Brook Trail. Part of the original loop turned right into Arnos Park. Road walking now you pass near to Alexandra Palace and Wood Green and onto Hornsey. The river beyond through Harringay has no path and you walk along Wightman Road and past Harringay West Station to Finsbury Park. Here you turn left and then right into the park to rejoin the river. Less than a mile later you walk by the river with the East and West Reservoirs on your left - particularly attractive section and part of the Capital Ring walk.

Gaining the road with Manor House Tube Station to the right, you turn left past the Castle Climbing Centre, a former pumping station with the Stoke Newington Filter Beds opposite - closed in 1991. Continue into Clissold Park, from here onwards the river is piped underground as you walk along Petherton Road. Keeping straight ahead you gain Colebrook Row and final stages of the New River path. You cross the road near the Angel Tube Station and pass the back of Sadlers Wells Theatre before turning right through the aptly named,

Myddleton Passage, to reach the viewing platform of the New River and Pump House on the right.

New River Head 1752 - Photo information board at the present viewing area at the New River Head.

WALK RECORD PAGE

Date walked -

Forty Hall, Cheshunt and New River - 7 miles ....

Whitewebbs and Crews Hill - 7 1/2 miles ....

Wormley Wood & Goff's Oak - 6 miles ....

Wormley West End & Brickendon - 6 1/2 miles ....

Wormelbury & Ermine Street - 6 miles ....

Ermine Street & Hertford Heath - 6 miles ....

Rye House, New River & Haileybury - 8 miles ....

River Lee Navigation & New River - 10 miles ....

Brickendon, Bayford and Hertford - 8 miles ....

Hertford Heath, Great Amwell & New River - 8 miles ....

New River - Forty Hill (A10) to Islington - 16 miles ....

THE JOHN MERRILL WALK BADGE

Complete six walks in this book and get the above special embroidered
badge and signed certificate. Badges are Black cloth
with lettering and hiker embroidered in four colours.

BADGE ORDER FORM

Date walks completed...

NAME ....

ADDRESS ....

....

Price: £6.00 each including postage, packing, VAT and signed completion
certificate. Amount enclosed (Payable to The John Merrill Foundation).

HAPPY WALKING T SHIRT - £7.50 ALL sizes.
From: The John Merrill Foundation,
32, Holmesdale, Waltham Cross,
Hertsfordshire, EN8 8QY

Tel - 01992 - 762776   Fax - +44(0)870 131 5061
E-mail - marathonhiker@aol.com

Order on line - www.johnmerrillwalkguides.com

********** YOU MAY PHOTOCOPY THIS FORM **********

EQUIPMENT NOTES
.....some personal thoughts from John N. Merrill

Today there is a bewildering variety of walking gear, much is superfluous to general walking in Britain. As a basic observation, people over dress for the outdoors. Basically equipment should be serviceable and do the task. I don't approve of or use walking poles; humans were built to walk with two legs! The following are some of my throughts gathered from my walking experiences.

BOOTS - For summer use and day walking I wear lightweight boots. For high mountains and longer trips I prefer a good quality boot with a full leather upper, of medium weight, with a vibram sole. I always add a foam cushioned insole to help cushion the base of my feet. Contary to popular belief, I do not use nor recommend Merrell footwear!

SOCKS - I generally wear two thick pairs as this helps minimise blisters. The inner pair are of loop stitch variety and approximately 80% wool. The outer are a thick rib pair of approximately 80% wool.

CLOTHES & WATERPROOFS - for general walking I wear a T shirt or cotton shirt with a cotton wind jacket on top, and shorts - even in snow! You generate heat as you walk and I prefer to layer my clothes to avoid getting too hot. Depending on the season will dictate how many layers you wear. In soft rain I just use my wind jacket for I know it quickly dries out. In heavy or consistant rain I slip on a poncho, which covers my pack and allows air to circulate, while keeping dry. Only in extreme conditions will I don overtrousers, much preferring to get wet and feel comfortable. I never wear gaiters, except when cross country skiing, in snow and glacier crossings.

FOOD - as I walk I carry bars of chocolate, for they provide instant energy and are light to carry. In winter a flask of hot coffee is welcome. I never carry water and find no hardship from not doing so, but this is a personal matter! From experience I find the more I drink the more I want and sweat. You should always carry some extra food such as trail mix & candy bars etc., for emergencies.

RUCKSACKS - for day walking I use a climbing rucksack of about 40 litre capacity and although it leaves excess space it does mean that the sac is well padded, with an internal frame and padded shoulder straps. Inside apart from the basics for one day, in winter I carry gloves, wear a hat and carry a spare pullover and a pair of socks.

MAP & COMPASS - when I am walking I always have the relevant map - preferably 1:25,000 scale - open in my hand. This enables me to constantly check that I am walking the right way. In case of bad weather I carry a compass, which once mastered gives you complete confidence in thick cloud or mist - you should always know where you are.

Why I walk

I am often asked why I walk and to be truthfull it is not easy to answer. I believe that walking gives you total freedom and at the same time getting some exercise without causing injuries like jogging. Freedom means the choice of walking at your own pace through a variety of countryside and looking and learning its secrets as you pass through. Freedom means the basics of life and you are master of your own destiny.

When I set off for the day I carry all I need on my back, be it for a day walk or an extended walk over days or months. I leave behind the trappings of modern life and break many of the accepted rules of walking, by walking alone, not informing anyone of where I am going and what my expected return is. I feel such niceties are restrictive and hinder one's freedom to dwell on places or extend the walk. I admit one must be careful and if conditions detrioate one must descend or seek shelter. Walking alone and facing the problems on the way enable one to know oneself totally and know how one reacts to situations and one's limitations. I don't carry a mobile phone for this is a trapping of modern life. To be out walking in solitude and suddenly the phone rings is an alarming thought; how can one be at peace with the countryside?

I walk not just for health but to see and explore an area of countryside. To follow a path by a stream and see a kingfisher flash by, or watch a dipper bobbing up and down on a rock are one of the delights and enchanting moments on a walk. To walk in Spring and see the different flowers emerging, the birds gathering twigs for their nests, the trees in bud and new leaves unfolding bring added pleasure to the scene. To walk into a village and look at the houses as you past, see the date stone or see a cheese press or stocks help to bring the village alive and see its past history. To look at the hall or other principal building, the inn with an unusual name makes one want to know more and perhaps at a later date a visit to the local history department of the nearby library to discover more. The church - the open book of village life - always deserves exploration. To wander around the gravestones and see the dates and inscriptions. To walk inside and see the ancient font or old tomb gives greater understanding to the walk.

I walk in the minimum of clothes for freedom. Only in winter do I wear long trousers preferring to wear shorts and a T shirt most of the time. Even in rain I prefer walking in shorts with a poncho keeping dry but allowing maximum movement and freedom. Boots are worn whatever the walk but a lightweight

61

pair for use in a dry summer and a more heavier and leather boot for winter or rain. A camera and binoculars to record and see distant mountains or birds; and for seeking out the blazed route ahead or for locating a stile.

Whilst there is the undeniable joy of exploring the area being walked through there is the added challenge of effort and fitness. I don't believe I walk fast just a steady 3 miles (5km) per hour, which I maintain without a rest during the day. I walk anything between 8 to 12 hours everyday, for days on end. I enjoy the mastery of walking up hill and dale and being able to push myself to walk further. Alternatively knowing I have thirty miles to walk, that day, and being able to pace oneself and complete the task still feeling fit and no pain. Knowing also that I can walk further if necessary. I don't train for a long walk simply preferring to set off and walk myself in as I progress.

Walking is spiritual. Yes, I believe in God and I have prayed often on a walk for help and guidance and have never been let down. I have also thanked him for the wonders I have seen on the way. Who cannot be moved when ascending to a pass and seeing sprawled out before you some incredibly beautiful scene. Who can wonder that after ten days alone in the wilderness that I reach the precise point I have been walking to. Yes, it is skill but I have been helped along the way and "shown" the route.

Walking is addictive but not compulsive. I find no hardship in walking day after day a marathon or more with forty pounds or more on my back. I never want to give up and can't wait to start again in the morning. The return from a long walk means a day walk has little meaning and for a while I peer out of the window but find it hard to put on the boots. But after a while as I have readjusted back a little I become restless and "angry" and put the boots on and walk for a few hours. If after that I have not been out for a few days I start to get withdrawal symptoms and have to break free and go for a walk.

So walking for me is a way of life, giving me the freedom to explore the countryside at my own pace. No other hobby or job gives you so much - exercise, experience, delight, discovery, adventure and exploration at such a minimal cost. It is man's simplest form of travel - on foot - and the only way to explore the world.

My footprint.

OTHER NORTH LONDON WALK BOOKS
by JOHN N. MERRILL

SHORT CIRCULAR WALKS ON THE RIVER LEE NAVIGATION - Northern Volume - Ponder's End - Hertford. 64 pages, 23 photographs, 10 detailed maps and walks. History notes.
- ISBN 1-903627-68-0 @ £8.50
WALKING THE RIVER LEE NAVIGATION - VOL 1 & 2.

SHORT CIRCULAR WALKS ON THE NEW RIVER & SOUTH EAST HERTFORDSHIRE
11 walks - 5 to 10 miles long between Waltham Cross and Hertford; many on the New River. New revised and enlarged edition 80 pages, 24 photographs, 13 detailed maps. History notes.
ISBN 1-903627-69-9 @ £8.95

SHORT CIRCULAR WALKS IN EPPING FOREST
10 circular walks 6 to 18 miles long. Combined they explore the whole forest and its surrounding area. 68 pages. 12 maps. 30 photographs. History notes.
ISBN 1-903627-72-9 @ £8.50

LONG CIRCULAR WALKS IN EASTERN HERTFORDSHIRE
9 walks - 15 to 20 miles long. Beautiful unspoilt walking in rolling countryside full of historical interest. £10.95
ISBN 978-0-9553691-7-9

LONG CIRCULAR WALKS IN WESTERN HERTFORDSHIRE -
9 long walks - 15 to 20 miles.. 112 pages. Wire bound. 55 photographs. 20 detailed maps. £10.95
ISBN 978-0-955651113

SHORT CIRCULAR WALKS AROUND HERTFORD.
3 historical Town walks and four country walks.
ISBN 978-0-9556511-7-5 £9.95

NEW - SHORT CIRCULAR WALKS AROUND BISHOP' STORTFORD

SHORT CIRCULAR WALKS ON THE RIVER STORT NAVIGATION
8 circular walks; 1 End to End walk. Full history and photographic study of this peaceful waterway. 92 pages. 68 photographgs. 12 maps. ISBN 1-903627- 73-7 £11.95

SHORT CIRCULAR WALKS ON THE RIVER LEE NAVIGATION - Southern Volume -
Limehouse basin to Hackney Marsh. 5 walks on the Regent Canal, Hertford Union and Limehouse Cut. Including Three Mills and its rivers. The guide also details a 28 mile End to End walk along the Navigation. 68 pages. 10 maps, 30 photographs.
ISBn 1-903627-74-5 £7.95

EPPING FOREST CHALLENGE WALK - 21 MILES.
Starts and ends at Waltham Abbey and takes in the whole forest. 44 pages. 6 maps. 10 photos £7.95
ISBN 978-0-9553691-0-0

"St. ALBANS WAY" - 26 mile Pilgrims walk from Waltham Abbey to St. Alban's Cathedral.
£7.95
ISBN 978-0-9553691-3-1

NORTH LONDON - THE THREE BOROUGH CHALLENGE WALK - 21 MILES
A walk linking together the three boroughs of Enfield, Barnet and Haringey.
A magnificent countryside walk. Certificate for the successful.
A5. 40 pages. Full colour book. ISBN 978-0-9556511-9-9
£7.95

NEW - SHORT CIRCULAR WALKS IN EPPING DISTRICT

NEW LONDON WALK GUIDES

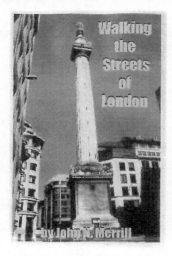

WALKING THE CANALS OF LONDON

Nine walks fully exploring - The Regents Canal, Grand Union Canal (Paddington Branch), River Thames and Isle of Dogs and the "London Canal Loop".
A5 wire bound. 108 pages. 13 maps. 95 b/w photographs.

£10.95   ISBN 978-0-9553691-2-4

WALKING THE STREETS OF LONDON

7 historical short walks - 2 to 6 miles long and allowing - 4 TO 5 HOURS - in the city with basic themes -

*"The Great Fire', "Wigs & Pens". The Good and Gracious".
"The Royal Palaces", "The Hot Spots", "Bridges, Boats and Dungeons".
"Monks, murder, punishment and poetry".*

A5 wire bound. 112 pages. 9 maps. 84 b/w photographs.

£10.95   ISBN 978-0-9553691-1-7

LONDON INTERFAITH WALKS

Seven walks in London to all the major religious sites.
Themed walks - Christian, Buddhist, Hindu etc.
. A5 Wire bound. 112 pages. 10 maps   130 photos.
   £10.95
ISBN 978-0-9568044-3-3

**See all our books on our
website -
www.johnmerrillwalkguides.com**

OTHER JOHN MERRILL WALK BOOKS

<u>CIRCULAR WALK GUIDES -</u>
SHORT CIRCULAR WALKS IN THE PEAK DISTRICT - Vol. 1,2, 3 AND 9
CIRCULAR WALKS IN WESTERN PEAKLAND
SHORT CIRCULAR WALKS IN THE STAFFORDSHIRE MOORLANDS
SHORT CIRCULAR WALKS - TOWNS & VILLAGES OF THE PEAK DISTRICT
SHORT CIRCULAR WALKS AROUND MATLOCK
SHORT CIRCULAR WALKS IN "PEAK PRACTICE COUNTRY."
SHORT CIRCULAR WALKS IN THE DUKERIES
SHORT CIRCULAR WALKS IN SOUTH YORKSHIRE
SHORT CIRCULAR WALKS IN SOUTH DERBYSHIRE
SHORT CIRCULAR WALKS AROUND BUXTON
SHORT CIRCULAR WALKS AROUND WIRKSWORTH
SHORT CIRCULAR WALKS IN THE HOPE VALLEY
40 SHORT CIRCULAR WALKS IN THE PEAK DISTRICT
CIRCULAR WALKS ON KINDER & BLEAKLOW
SHORT CIRCULAR WALKS IN SOUTH NOTTINGHAMSHIRE
SHORT CIRCULAR WALKS IN CHESHIRE
SHORT CIRCULAR WALKS IN WEST YORKSHIRE
WHITE PEAK DISTRICT AIRCRAFT WRECKS
CIRCULAR WALKS IN THE DERBYSHIRE DALES
SHORT CIRCULAR WALKS FROM BAKEWELL
SHORT CIRCULAR WALKS IN LATHKILL DALE
CIRCULAR WALKS IN THE WHITE PEAK
SHORT CIRCULAR WALKS IN EAST DEVON
SHORT CIRCULAR WALKS AROUND HARROGATE
SHORT CIRCULAR WALKS IN CHARNWOOD FOREST
SHORT CIRCULAR WALKS AROUND CHESTERFIELD
SHORT CIRCULAR WALKS IN THE YORKS DALES - Vol 1 - SOUTHERN AREA
SHORT CIRCULAR WALKS IN THE AMBER VALLEY (DERBYSHIRE)
SHORT CIRCULAR WALKS IN THE LAKE DISTRICT
SHORT CIRCULAR WALKS IN THE NORTH YORKSHIRE MOORS
SHORT CIRCULAR WALKS IN EAST STAFFORDSHIRE
LONG CIRCULAR WALKS IN THE PEAK DISTRICT - Vol.1, 2 , 3 , 4 AND 5.
DARK PEAK AIRCRAFT WRECK WALKS
LONG CIRCULAR WALKS IN THE STAFFORDSHIRE MOORLANDS
LONG CIRCULAR WALKS IN CHESHIRE
WALKING THE TISSINGTON TRAIL
WALKING THE HIGH PEAK TRAIL
WALKING THE MONSAL TRAIL & SETT VALLEY TRAILS
PEAK DISTRICT WALKING - TEN "TEN MILER'S" - Vol One AND Two
CLIMB THE PEAKS OF THE PEAK DISTRICT
PEAK DISTRICT WALK A MONTH Vols One,Two, Three, Four, Five & Six
TRAIN TO WALK Vol. One - The Hope Valley Line
DERBYSHIRE LOST VILLAGE WALKS -Vol One and Two.
CIRCULAR WALKS IN DOVEDALE AND THE MANIFOLD VALLEY
WALKING AROUND GLOSSOP
WALKING THE LONGDENDALE TRAIL
WALKING THE UPPER DON TRAIL
SHORT CIRCULAR WALKS IN CANNOCK CHASE
CIRCULAR WALKS IN THE DERWENT VALLEY
WALKING THE TRAILS OF NORTH-EAST DERBYSHIRE
WALKING THE PENNINE BRIDLEWAY & CIRCULAR WALKS
SHORT CIRCULAR WALKS ON THE NEW RIVER & SOUTH-EAST HERTFORDSHIRE
SHORT CIRCULAR WALKS IN EPPING FOREST
WALKING THE STREETS OF LONDON
LONG CIRCULAR WALKS IN EASTERN HERTFORDSHIRE
LONG CIRCULAR WALKS IN WESTERN HERTFORDSHIRE
WALKS IN THE LONDON BOROUGH OF ENFIELD
WALKS IN THE LONDON BOROUGH OF BARNET
WALKS IN THE LONDON BOROUGH OF HARINGEY
WALK IN THE LONDON BOROUGH OF WALTHAM FOREST
SHORT CIRCULAR WALKS AROUND HERTFORD
THE BIG WALKS OF LONDON
SHORT CIRCULAR WALKS AROUND BISHOP'S STORTFORD
SHORT CIRCULAR WALKS AROUND EPPING DISTRICT
CIRCULAR WALKS IN THE BOROUGH OF BROXBOURNE
LONDON INTERFAITH WALKS
LONG CIRCULAR WALKS IN THE NORTH CHILTERNS

For a free complete catalogue of John Merrill walk Guides send a SAE to The John Merrill Foundation

<u>CANAL WALKS -</u>
VOL 1 - DERBYSHIRE & NOTTINGHAMSHIRE
VOL 2 - CHESHIRE & STAFFORDSHIRE
VOL 3 - STAFFORDSHIRE
VOL 4 - THE CHESHIRE RING
VOL 5 - THE GRANTHAM CANAL
VOL 6 - SOUTH YORKSHIRE
VOL 7 - THE TRENT & MERSEY CANAL
VOL 8 - WALKING THE DERBY CANAL RING
VOL 9 - WALKING THE LLANGOLLEN CANAL
VOL 10 - CIRCULAR WALKS ON THE CHESTERFIELD CANAL
VOL 11 - CIRCULAR WALKS ON THE CROMFORD CANAL
Vol.13 - SHORT CIRCULAR WALKS ON THE RIVER LEE NAVIGATION -Vol. 1 - NORTH
Vol. 14 - SHORT CIRCULAR WALKS ON THE RIVER STORT NAVIGATION
Vol.15 - SHORT CIRCULAR WALKS ON THE RIVER LEE NAVIGATION - Vol. 2 - SOUTH
Vol. 16 - WALKING THE CANALS OF LONDON
Vol 17 - WALKING THE RIVER LEE NAVIGATION
Vol. 20 - SHORT CIRCULAR WALKS IN THE COLNE VALLEY
Vol 21 - THE BLACKWATER & CHELMER NAVIGATION - End to End.

Visit our website -
www.johnmerrillwalkguides.com

<u>JOHN MERRILL DAY CHALLENGE WALKS -</u>
WHITE PEAK CHALLENGE WALK
THE HAPPY HIKER - WHITE PEAK - CHALLENGE WALK No.2
DARK PEAK CHALLENGE WALK
PEAK DISTRICT END TO END WALKS
STAFFORDSHIRE MOORLANDS CHALLENGE WALK

THE LITTLE JOHN CHALLENGE WALK
YORKSHIRE DALES CHALLENGE WALK
NORTH YORKSHIRE MOORS CHALLENGE WALK
LAKELAND CHALLENGE WALK
THE RUTLAND WATER CHALLENGE WALK
MALVERN HILLS CHALLENGE WALK
THE SALTER'S WAY
THE SNOWDON CHALLENGE
CHARNWOOD FOREST CHALLENGE WALK
THREE COUNTIES CHALLENGE WALK (PEAK DISTRICT).
CAL-DER-WENT WALK BY GEOFFREY CARR,
THE QUANTOCK WAY
BELVOIR WITCHES CHALLENGE WALK
THE CARNEDDAU CHALLENGE WALK
THE SWEET PEA CHALLENGE WALK
THE LINCOLNSHIRE WOLDS - BLACK DEATH - CHALLENGE WALK
JENNIFER'S CHALLENGE WALK
THE EPPING FOREST CHALLENGE WALK
THE THREE BOROUGH CHALLENGE WALK - NORTH LONDON

INSTRUCTION & RECORD -
HIKE TO BE FIT......STROLLING WITH JOHN
THE JOHN MERRILL WALK RECORD BOOK
HIKE THE WORLD - JOHN MERRILL'S GUIDE TO WALKING & BACKPACKING.

MULTIPLE DAY WALKS -
THE RIVERS'S WAY
PEAK DISTRICT: HIGH LEVEL ROUTE
PEAK DISTRICT: MARATHONS
THE LIMEY WAY
THE PEAKLAND WAY
COMPO'S WAY BY ALAN HILEY
THE BRIGHTON WAY BY NORMAN WILLIS

THE PILGRIM WALKS SERIES -
THE WALSINGHAM WAY - ELY TO WALSINGHAM - 72 MILES
THE WALSINGHAM WAY - KINGS LYNN TO WALSINGHAM - 35 MILES
TURN LEFT AT GRANJA DE LA MORERUELA - 700 MILES
NORTH TO SANTIAGO DE COMPOSTELA, VIA FATIMA - 650 MILES
ST. OLAV'S WAY - OSLO TO TRONDHEIM - 400 MILES
ST. WINEFRIDE'S WAY - ST. ASAPH TO HOLYWELL
ST. ALBANS WAY - WALTHAM ABBEY TO ST. ALBANS - 26 MILES
ST. KENELM TRAIL BY JOHN PRICE - CLENT HILLS TO WINCHCOMBE - 60 MILES
DERBYSHIRE PILGRIMAGES
LONDON TO CANTERBURY- 75 MILES
LONDON TO ST. ALBANS - 36 MILES
LONDON TO WALSINGHAM - 194 MILES
FOLKESTONE, HYTHE TO CANTERBURY - 25 MILES
THE JOHN SCHORNE PEREGRINATIONS - 27 MILES BY M. MOONEY
ST CEDD'S PILGRIMAGE WALK - 24 MILES
ST BIRINIUS PILGRIMAGE WALK - 26 MILES
OUR LADY OF ULTING PILGRIMAGE WALK - 16 MILES
OUR LADY OF CAVERSHAM PILGRIMAGE WALK - 38 MILES
THE MANDEVILLE MONKS WAY - 32 MILES
THE ESSEX PRIORIES WAY - 20 MILES

COAST WALKS & NATIONAL TRAILS -
ISLE OF WIGHT COAST PATH
PEMBROKESHIRE COAST PATH
THE CLEVELAND WAY
WALKING ANGLESEY'S COASTLINE.
WALKING THE COASTLINE OF THE CHANNEL ISLANDS
THE ISLE OF MAN COASTAL PATH - "THE WAY OF THE GULL."
A WALK AROUND HAYLING ISLAND
A WALK AROUND THE ISLE OF SHEPPEY
A WALK AROUND THE ISLE OF JERSEY
WALKING AROUND THE ISLANDS OF ESSEX

DERBYSHIRE & PEAK DISTRICT HISTORICAL GUIDES -
A TO Z GUIDE OF THE PEAK DISTRICT
DERBYSHIRE INNS - AN A TO Z GUIDE
HALLS AND CASTLES OF THE PEAK DISTRICT & DERBYSHIRE
TOURING THE PEAK DISTRICT & DERBYSHIRE BY CAR
DERBYSHIRE FOLKLORE
PUNISHMENT IN DERBYSHIRE
CUSTOMS OF THE PEAK DISTRICT & DERBYSHIRE
WINSTER - A SOUVENIR GUIDE
ARKWRIGHT OF CROMFORD
LEGENDS OF DERBYSHIRE
DERBYSHIRE FACTS & RECORDS
TALES FROM THE MINES BY GEOFFREY CARR
PEAK DISTRICT PLACE NAMES BY MARTIN SPRAY
DERBYSHIRE THROUGH THE AGES - VOL 1 -DERBYSHIRE IN PREHISTORIC TIMES
SIR JOSEPH PAXTON
FLORENCE NIGHTINGALE
JOHN SMEDLEY
BONNIE PRINCE CHARLIE & 20 MILE WALK.
THE STORY OF THE EARLS AND DUKES OF DEVONSHIRE

JOHN MERRILL'S MAJOR WALKS -
TURN RIGHT AT LAND'S END
WITH MUSTARD ON MY BACK
TURN RIGHT AT DEATH VALLEY
EMERALD COAST WALK
I CHOSE TO WALK - WHY I WALK ETC.
A WALK IN OHIO - 1,310 MILES AROUND THE BUCKEYE TRAIL.

SKETCH BOOKS -
SKETCHES OF THE PEAK DISTRICT

COLOUR BOOK:-
THE PEAK DISTRICT.......SOMETHING TO REMEMBER HER BY.

OVERSEAS GUIDES -
HIKING IN NEW MEXICO - VOL I - THE SANDIA AND MANZANO MOUNTAINS.
VOL 2 - HIKING "BILLY THE KID" COUNTRY. VOL 4 - N.W. AREA - " HIKING INDIAN COUNTRY."
"WALKING IN DRACULA COUNTRY" - ROMANIA.
WALKING THE TRAILS OF THE HONG KONG ISLANDS.

VISITOR GUIDES - MATLOCK . BAKEWELL. ASHBOURNE.

THE PILGRIM'S WAY SERIES
by Revd. John N. Merrill

THE WALSINGHAM WAY
- Ely to Walsingham - 72 miles - 1-903627-33-8 ....£8.95
- 56 pages and 40 photographs.

THE WALSINGHAM WAY
- King's Lynn to Walsingham - 35 miles - 1-903627-41 - 9 ....£9.95
- 72 pages and 50 colour photographs.

TURN LEFT AT GRANJA DE LA MORERUELA
- 700 miles - Seville to Santiago de Compostela, Spain. 1-903627 - 40 - 0 ....£14.95..
- 172 pages and 120 photographs

NORTH TO SANTIAGO DE COMPOSTELA VIA FATIMA -
1-903627- 44- 3 - 650 miles from Lagos, Algarve, through Portugal via Fatima to Santiago de Compostela.........£17.95.. - 220 pages and 160 photographs

ST. OLAV'S WAY - 400 MILES - NORWAY
- Photgraphic book and basic guide ...1 - 903627- 45 - 1...........£12.95
- 124 pages and 130 photographs.

ST. WINEFRIDE'S WAY - 14 miles - St. Asaph to Holywell.
ISBN 1-903627-66-4   40 pages. 5 maps. 20 photographs..£6.95

ST. ALBAN'S WAY - 25 mile walk from Waltham Abbey to St. Alban's Cathedral.
Linking together two major medieval pilgrimage centres.
ISBN 978-0-9553691-3-1 48 Pages. 7 maps. 18 colour photographs. £7.95

ST. KENELM'S TRAIL by John Price - From the Clent Hills to Winchcombe Abbey - 60 miles. ISBN 978-0-9553691-6-2. 60 pages 5 maps....£7.50

DERBYSHIRE PILGRIMAGES - The pilgrimage routes, saints and hermits of the county and Peak District. Plus a St. Bertram Walk and about a pilgrimage.
48 pages. £5.95

LONDON TO ST. ALBANS - 36 MILES ......NEW....... ISBN 978-0-9560649-7-4
80 pages. Wire bound. 45 photos. 8 maps. A stunning walk from Westminster to St. Albans via 32 churches. £9.95

FOLKESTONE, HYTHE TO CANTERBURY - 25 MILES ..NEW
ISBN 9780956064981.............68 pages. 40 colour phots. 8 maps. £9.95

LONDON TO CANTERBURY - 75 MILES.
ISBN 9780956064967 140 pages. 146 PHOTOS. 15 maps...................£12.95

LONDON TO WALSINGHAM - 190 MILES
ISBN 9780956464422..................256pages. 250 photos. 40 maps. ...£14.95

THE JOHN SCHORNE PEREGRINATION by Michael Mooney. 27 mile walk in Buckinghamshire to North Marston, the site of medieval miracles and pilgrimage.
A5. 56 pages. 16 colour photographs. 8 maps. £7.95
ISBN 978-0-9564644-0-8

ST CEDD'S PILGRIMAGE - 24 MILES -To St. Peter's Chapel on the Wall, near Bradwell on Sea. ISBN 978-0-9564644-7-7. 56 pages. A5 24 colour photos. 4 maps. £6.94

ST BIRINIUS PILGRIMAGE - 26 MILES - To his shrine in Dorchester Abbey, Oxfordshire.
ISBN 978-0-9564644-8-4 56 pages. 20 colour photos. 8 maps. £6.95

PILGRIM'S PASSPORT - ISBN 978-0-9568044-1-9 Specially designed book to record your sello's. £5.00

OUR LADY OF ULTING PILGRIMAGE WALK - 16 MILES - To a former Marian shrine is Essex, near Maldon. ISBN 978-0-9568044-5-7 £6.95

OUR LADY OF CAVERSHAM PILGRIMAGE WALK - 38 MILES - Windsor to Reading.

MANDEVILLE MONKS WAY - 42 MILES - Edmonton Green (N. Lopndon) to Saffron Walden.

THE ESSEX PRIORY WAY - 20 MILES - St. Osyth to Colchester, linking St/ Osyth Priory and St. Botoloph's Priory together. Beautiful coastal walk. ISBN 978-0-9568044-8-8

see my website - **www.pilgrimways.co.uk**

Illustrated Lectures include -

" WALKING AROUND LONDON" - a brief look at walking in the city and countryside around London, some 1,800 miles of walking. - Capital Ring, Canals, London Loop, River Thames, New River, Pymmes Brook Trail & Jubilee Walkway, The Wandle Trail, the River Stort and Lee Navigations and Lee Valley Walk.

"WALKING MY WAY" - Why I walk and some of walks I have done - a hilarious but exhausting talk, from more than 182,000 miles of walking!

"WALKING THE CHESOPEAKE & OHIO CANAL - 250 miles from Washington D.C. to Cumberland, Maryland, USA.

"NORTH TO SANTIAGO via FATIMA" - 650 mile pilgrim's walk to Santiago de Compostelo, through Portugal.

"FOLLOW THE BLUE BLAZE" - Walking around the Buckeye Trail in Ohio, USA. 1,300 miles - the first person to walk the complete trail in one continuous walk.

"Promoting walking, Pilgrimages, and understanding the countryside."

HOW TO DO A WALK

The walk in this book follows a public right of way, be it a footpath, bridleway, Boat or RUPP, which are marked in green lines on the Ordnance Survey 1:25,000 Explorer maps.

On each section I have detailed which map is needed and I would urge you to carry and use the map. As I walk I always have the map out on the section I am walking, constantly checking that I am walking the right way. Also when coming to any road or path junction, I can check on the map to ensure I take the right route.

Most the paths are signed and waymarked with coloured arrows but I would at best describe them as intermittent. They act as confirmation of the right of way you are walking and the arrow points in the direction of travel.

The countryside has the added problem of vandalism and you will find path logo's and Information Boards spray painted over and path signs pointing the wrong way! That is why I always advise carrying the map open on the area you are walking to check you are walking the right way. In my walking instructions I have given the name of each main and minor road, canal lock, and bridge, together with the house numbers where you turn and the name of inns passed. All to help you have a smooth and trouble free walk.

I confirm I have walked every route and written what I found at the time of walking.

These comments are not meant to put you off but to make you aware of some of the problems of walking in the countryside.

THE JOHN MERRILL MINISTRY

— *Embracing & honouring all faiths.*

John has been following his own spiritual path all his life, and is guided. He was brought up as a Christian and confirmed at the age of 13. He then went to a Quaker Boarding School for five years and developed his love for the countryside and walking. He became fascinated with Tibet and whilst retaining his Christian roots, became immersed in Buddhism. For four years he studied at the Tara Buddhist Centre in Derbyshire. He progressed into Daoism and currently attends the Chinese Buddhist Temple (Pure Land Tradition) in London. With his thirst for knowledge and discovery he paid attention to other faiths and appreciated their values. Late in life he decided it was time to reveal his spiritual beliefs and practices and discovered the Interfaith Seminary.

"When the pupil is ready, the teacher will appear". (Buddhist saying).

Here for two years he learnt in more depth the whole spectrum of faiths , including Jainism, Paganism, Mother Earth, Buddhism, Hinduism, Islam, Judaism, Sikhism, Celtic Worship and Shamanism. This is an ongoing exploration without end. He embraces all faiths, for all have a beauty of their own. All paths/faiths lead to one goal/truth. On July 17th. 2010 he was Ordained as an Interfaith Minister.

*"May you go in peace, with joy in your heart
and may the divine be always at your side."*

Using his knowledge and experience he combines many faiths into a simple, caring and devoted services, individually made for each specific occasion, with dignity and honour. He conducts special Ceremonies -

*** Funerals   * Weddings   *Civil Partnerships * Baby Blessings & Naming
* Rites of Passage * Healing Ceremonies * Pilgimages * Inspirational Talks**

**For further information Contact John on -
Tel/Fax: 01992 - 762776
Email - marathonhiker@aol.com
Ministry site -www.pilgrimways.co.uk**

*For more infomation about Interfaith work see -
www.interfaithfoundation.org*

**Revd. John N. Merrill, HonMUni, R.I.M.A.
32, Holmesdale, Waltham Cross, Hertfordshire EN8 8QY**

As I walk ....

I am not aware of my feet touching the earth, but am always looking ahead surveying the ground and intuitively place my feet where necessary. I look at all my surroundings, the hedges, trees, flowers and stop and observe the birds and animals that cross my path.

I see the wren calling in the hedgerows. I see the wild flowers growing throughout the seasons. I hear the call of a green woodpecker that sweeps ahead of me across the field. I near a scratching squirrel and call to it and watch him watching me briefly, before running and leaping effortless to a tree and up its bark. I follow and watch him hiding and ascending the tree, before swinging off onto another tree branch. I surprise a pheasant, who surprises us both and shrieks taking to the air urgently. I stop and admire a bee orchid growing alone on the field edge, knowing it is rare and must not be picked, for it will die.

I follow the path down to a brook and cross the footbridge and stop and gaze at the water to see if anything moves here or along the banks. Sometimes I see a fish, a water vole and occasionally a kingfisher - a mere flash of blue, but nevertheless a wondrous sight. I walk further and as I round a bend in the path in woodland, I surprise six roe deer who prick their ears, snort, and run away only to stop moments later to look again at this intruder in their world.

I marvel at these sights and sounds, which make me both joyful and humble at seeing the living unspoilt world, of which we all connected.

I walk beside a barbed wire fence and notice the sheep's wool caught on the barbs, as they either squeezed through or reached for a succulent piece of grass.

I watch the trees sway in the light breeze, the leaves flutter gently. I gaze at the fluffy clouds that glide across the sky. I walk in the cool damp air, but all is enjoyable and serene. Then suddenly the sun appears, and for a brief moment, illuminates my world and can see everything in its vibrant colours. As though showing me what is there and be patient. The clouds roll in and I am left with the magic of those priceless seconds. My heart is full of love for sharing this moment.

I walk on just looking and admiring all that my eyes see. I know I am guided and watched over, for I never put a foot wrong. I just walk with no preconceived ideas and no expectations. I just let it all happened in its own good time, which makes me very blessed at what has occurred.

I visit a church and are humbled at the workmanship and the story of the woodwork, stone and memorials. I touch the font and feel its story and energy.

As I walk though woodland and stop and rest by an oak tree and feel its trunk against my back. I feel its energy and wisdom, and say a prayer and touch it gently with my hand.

As I near the end of the walk I turn and raise my hand and say good-bye and thanks for allowing me to visit and enjoy your surroundings. It has meant much and I shall return to explore further and watch the unfolding kaleidoscope of life that exists there.

I walk and give thanks that I am able to do so with my body and mind. It is all a deep and profound experience without end.

© John Merrill - 9/2/2010